65083

W9-BZD-075

DATE			
WITHDRAWN			

BAKER & TAYLOR

Henry Clay the Lawyer

HENRY CLAY
THE LAWYER

Maurice G. Baxter

THE UNIVERSITY PRESS OF KENTUCKY

Publication of this volume was made possible in part
by a grant from the National Endowment for the Humanities.

Scholarly publisher for the Commonwealth,
serving Bellarmine College, Berea College, Centre
College of Kentucky, Eastern Kentucky University,
The Filson Club Historical Society, Georgetown College,
Kentucky Historical Society, Kentucky State University,
Morehead State University, Murray State University,
Northern Kentucky University, Transylvania University,
University of Kentucky, University of Louisville,
and Western Kentucky University.

Editorial and Sales Offices: The University Press of Kentucky
663 South Limestone Street, Lexington, Kentucky 40508-4008

04 03 02 01 00   5 4 3 2 1

Library of Congress Cataloging-in-Publication Data

Baxter, Maurice G. (Maurice Glen), 1920-
    Henry Clay the lawyer / Maurice G. Baxter.
        p.   cm.
    Includes bibliographical references and index.
    ISBN 0-8131-2147-7 (alk. paper)
    1. Clay, Henry, 1777-1852.   2. Lawyers—United States
Biography.   3. United States—Politics and government—
1815-1861.   I. Title.
KF368.C575B39   2000
340'.092—dc21   99-32612
[B]

This book is printed on acid-free recycled paper meeting
the requirements of the American National Standard
for Permanence of Paper for Printed Library Materials.

Manufactured in the United States of America

CONTENTS

PREFACE

Ever since the early nineteenth century when Henry Clay was prominent in American politics, many histories, biographies, and articles have described his public and private characteristics. None has fully focused on the Kentuckian's activity as a lawyer, though for more than fifty years he earned much of his living in the legal profession. During this half century, modern American law was taking shape, borrowing from English experience but developing new rules and precedents applicable to huge societal changes. Clay was an active participant in that process.

I have examined Clay's practice at levels from county and state jurisdictions to the Supreme Court and have drawn upon arguments by attorneys and opinions of judges, as well as the correspondence of Clay and others. The story is filled out from relevant historical sources, showing the economic and political setting. As an examination of constitutional and legal history, this study explores the broad scope and relevance of such a contextual approach. Investigating Clay's career in law as well as politics should provide useful perspectives.

As a youth in eastern Virginia, Henry was sent off by his parents to nearby Richmond, where he was placed with the learned Chancellor George Wythe as a clerk, a great opportunity to learn the basics of lawyering. Others who had profited from Wythe's instruction became leading figures in the republic: Thomas Jefferson, John Marshall, John Breckinridge, and others. So the question whether Clay's preparation was good can be answered yes. His reputation as a lawyer, of course, depended also upon his later professional performance. In the early years of his practice after arriving in Lexington, Kentucky, Clay quickly moved ahead in collecting debts for eastern merchants and in handling cases involving tangled land titles. Was his success due to his ability or simply to his personal connections with established lawyers? Or was it due to his marriage, which brought him into the family of the well-to-do Thomas Hart?

Rather soon he moved into the state's politics, the beginning of a life-long political career. As with others in similar situations, the roles of lawyer and politician were complementary. What effect did this combination of interests have upon his involvement in matters such as banking, both state and national? Were there objectionable aspects of these connections?

From the beginning of his legal career in 1798 and extending to the time of his death in 1852, Clay emphasized cases about land titles, which accounted for the greatest share of his professional income. Did this expertise contribute to his extensive involvement in congressional issues of public land policy, such as generous preemption by settlers and less generous distribution of proceeds from land sales to the states?

Increasingly, Clay the prominent politician and Clay the lawyer confronted issues about slavery. At first, they were questions of a local nature, but soon they involved broader issues attracting both his roles in politics and law. Such was true of his handling the important constitutional case of *Groves v Slaughter* (1841) concerning the interstate slave trade. Now he had moved to a conservative view on slavery, emphasizing concessions and compromises on this important subject in Congress. It was a revealing illustration of his position in court being affected by his position in politics. How much and with what effect those two elements of Clay's activity interacted are questions worth consideration in relation both to the general history of the nation and to republican principles. To understand his impact on his times and later institutions, it is also necessary to consider his personal traits. Unquestionably, he was gifted intellectually. And he knew it. Though not often, he could make sure that rivals and adversaries knew it too. Compared to other prominent figures of the day, he was unusually interested in reading materials related not only to the legal profession but also to advances in livestock breeding and horticulture, both of which he applied on his estate "Ashland." He was an authority on the important staple hemp, used for bagging southern cotton and making rope. And for much of his life he supported higher education at Transylvania University as legal counsel, faculty member, and trustee. In Congress he succeeded in getting legislation on the federal court system that required more judges and improved procedure.

Of course, Clay was not free of fault. As a young man, he was known for his hearty drinking and lively gambling habits. But as time passed, there was much less of this, notwithstanding rather fixed disapproving views of some historians, especially on his early years. He was prone to act from anger both in politics and in individual relations. For example, not long after he had clashed with opponents during debate in the state legislature, he became involved in an angry quarrel with his adversary, Humphrey Marshall, and challenged him to a duel. Fortunately the outcome on the field of honor across the Ohio River ended without much bloodshed. And after the disappointing presidential election of 1824, Clay challenged the erratic John Randolph to a duel, though this encounter, too, did not result in injury. In later years, Clay responded to perceived affronts with argument instead of risking physical confrontation.

This study of Clay's career as a lawyer begins with an account of the legal scene in which Clay operated, providing an overview of the court systems, federal and state, in which he practiced, and sketching the ideologies that shaped debates about the proper nature of American legal institutions. The study then examines Clay's early legal career, up to the period during and after the War of 1812, at which point his attention shifted for a decade or so to political affairs and away from the practice of law. The remainder of this book examines the particular areas in which Clay directed his later legal work: economic issues concerning land ownership, bankruptcy, and debt collection; banking matters pursued on behalf of the Bank of the United States and the Bank of Kentucky; and issues related to the legal status of the interstate slave trade. The study considers both the important constitutional cases in which Clay participated and also the far greater number of nonconstitutional cases in which he served as counsel. The picture that emerges from this study of Clay's career is one of a skilled lawyer influenced by his political commitments who addressed in an informed way the central legal and economic issues of his day.

I am greatly indebted to the editors of *The Papers of Henry Clay* (11 vols., University Press of Kentucky, 1959–1992) for their excellent collection of source materials and editorial annotations. I have drawn heavily upon them in this study, as my citations indicate. Noel Kinnamon provided excellent copyediting, and I am indebted to him for his contribution. As always, my wife, Cynthia Lewis Baxter, was involved through every stage of this enterprise. For this study I also received expert guidance and assistance from my son, Hugh Baxter.

1

∞

THE LEGAL SCENE

In 1792, when Henry Clay was a youth of fifteen, he had begun an apprenticeship in Virginia with the respected chancellor and professor of law, George Wythe. Here in Richmond reports of legal reform in the nation were arriving. Debate over legal reform was particularly lively in Kentucky, because at that time it was being detached as a new state from the Old Dominion. Across the mountains delegates were framing a state constitution, a process that generated spirited argument about fundamental principles of government. Though information about Henry's observations of what was occurring in this process has not survived, we know he could later recall this important process involving law and courts in the two states.

There were two opposing viewpoints in a rising debate about what shape the new Kentucky constitution should take. One was that of the radicals, advocating a bold extension of the heritage of the American Revolution, of sweeping change from excessive governmental power, from privileged classes, and from a legal system with elements of English common law. The other view was held by the moderates, who wanted gradual change, combining experience with old institutions and cautious reform. The radicals maintained that there was an undue influence by lawyers, belonging to an encrusted, untrustworthy profession. A republic, they believed, ought to reduce the dangerous political and social power of this elite group.

When the constitutional convention of 1792 assembled, the proceedings were already planned by George Nicholas, a moderate. Like young Clay, he had read law under Chancellor Wythe, as many others then did. Although Nicholas had only recently arrived in Kentucky, he presented a carefully planned agenda that showed promise of being adopted by the delegates. He wanted a government of balanced powers, including a judiciary that must check the operations of the other branches. At the top would be a court of appeals to monitor lower tribunals by reviewing their decisions. Furthermore, judges would have to be better qualified than many judges of that time. This appellate court would resolve land questions—indeed, Nicholas urged much attention to land law by all parts of the government, for that subject was central to the development of Kentucky's economy. And he pursued a policy stimulating commercial growth, which he thought was a primary support of the state. Here were connections of the economy with the law—perhaps natural connections for Nicholas, given his extensive financial interests in the state. Overall, Nicholas would borrow characteristics of the recently adopted United States Constitution. He also recommended adopting the common law of England, despite radical opposition, as well as continuing observance of the laws of Virginia in Kentucky. On this point there would be staunch disagreement. That would be true particularly in the future leading land case of *Green v Biddle* (1824) in the Supreme Court, one in which Clay would be much involved.

The convention was quite agreeable to Nicholas's agenda and approved it with few exceptions. He soon followed this triumph by smoothly managing the election of the first governor, Isaac Shelby, a revered pioneer and military veteran. Yet when the important question of land law arose, this explosive issue caused vigorous disagreement. Years earlier, the Virginia assembly had passed a law regulating acquisition and verification of land titles. A commission had adjudicated over 3,200 disputes, which were upheld by the supreme court of Virginia. Radicals in the Kentucky legislature and the appellate court were upset because claimants were not residents in their new state. The result was to stir up another radical-moderate battle, centering on the court system. Nicholas had lost some control of affairs.

A second constitutional convention was called in 1799. Lively debate on judicial reform followed but was crowded out of acceptance by a discussion of whether and how to adopt any change. John Breckinridge, Clay's good friend who was now the moderate leader, needed to give higher priority to endorsing and circulating the Jeffersonian resolution across the country condemning the federal sedition law passed the previous year. This situation allowed his opponents an opportunity to introduce different proposals.

One adversary, Felix Grundy, of the less-developed Green River area to the south, was tireless in behalf of his circuit-court plan with radical features. At last in 1802 he succeeded in getting the measure through but only over the governor's veto. Lawyers like Clay would have to argue cases before county district courts, partly composed of untrained assistants to circuit-riding judges. Moderates had little confidence in the capacity of these amateurs. Nevertheless, much of this judicial branch lasted at least until 1816. No doubt, moderates were somewhat consoled when they learned that similar radical movements in Massachusetts and Pennsylvania had been defeated.

The protracted conflict in Kentucky had been only one phase of the larger crisis concerning the relation of legal systems to republican government. Widespread dissatisfaction among Jeffersonians about law and lawyers, about their incompatibility with the people's fundamental values, would continue for a while. In Washington, President Jefferson and his extensive following were very troubled by decisions of the Supreme Court, particularly by the *Marbury* case (1803), advancing judicial review of congressional legislation, and also by the rulings in the chief justice's federal circuit court, blocking conviction of Aaron Burr for treason, and by the failed impeachment trial of Justice Samuel Chase in the Senate. It added up to strong political feeling about the administration of justice across the land. Was the cause of the problem an aggressive incursion against a democratic society? Even Henry Clay would ask similar questions when he worried about the impact of some decisions and policies.[1]

During this early period of the Supreme Court's history, lawyers significantly influenced the direction of American legal development. So in understanding what the Court ruled, one must take this factor into account. And in the early nineteenth century, the federal bar was composed of some interesting and gifted personalities. Among them certainly was William Pinkney, an eloquent, dandified figure, who was acknowledged to be in the front rank of constitutional lawyers. Among his impressive arguments was *McCulloch v Maryland* (1819), upholding the validity of the national bank's charter. Other notable figures were Thomas Emmet, an energetic Irish expatriate, and William Wirt, the United States attorney general for a long while.

In the view of many contemporaries, Daniel Webster became the head of the bar. His arguments for national powers and against state legislation, such as in the famous *Dartmouth College* case (1819), were generally in tune with the trend of John Marshall's court, but less so in the later Taney-Jacksonian years. He was co-counsel with Clay in several important arguments, including a number in behalf of the Bank of the United States and an interesting one concerning the interstate slave trade, *Groves v Slaughter* (1842).

In these early years many lawyers coming before the Court were easterners, due to arduous conditions of travel from other sections. There were quite a few, however, who could come because they were also members of Congress or had business with the government. Clay was one of this sort.

Procedures in hearings were less complicated than those today. Oral argument was a principal part of handling business.

Written briefs and even some court reports were less so. This encouraged long hours of lawyers' presentations and emphasized oratory, not a little entertainment for visitors who made their way down to a cramped courtroom in the Capitol's basement.[2] In framing briefs and making oral arguments, lawyers drew upon published legal authorities. Old English commentaries by Coke and Blackstone were continuing references, over which lawyers, such as Clay and Webster, had once struggled when entering practice. Like others, they now grounded cases also on American volumes by Joseph Story, St. George Tucker, and James Kent. By these routes English common law remained a staple in shaping materials for judges as well as attorneys. That bothered many critics, so much so that in a number of states, such as Kentucky, reformers sought to prohibit acceptance of this source, even in the form of citation by counsel. Clay did not support such a measure. In arguing a case in the Kentucky Court of Appeals, he suffered the judges' warning that he was prohibited from citing an English common law decision. He had knowingly done so, for he well remembered he had opposed passage of such a restriction when he had been a member of the state legislature. But in Marshall's Supreme Court there was no hindrance to reliance on those old materials. Besides, the federal courts had jurisdiction on questions of common law, conferred by congressional judiciary acts since 1789.[3]

Among the numerous persons serving as justices of this tribunal, Chief Justice John Marshall stands out as preeminent. He occupied the post for thirty-four years, as long as any other member of the Court. Appointed in 1801 by the outgoing Federalist President John Adams, he died in office in 1835. With little formal legal instruction, he spent only a few weeks under Wythe's guidance in Virginia and learned mostly on his own. He had the same connection with the eminent chancellor that Jefferson, Breckinridge, Clay, and many others had, though not all took the same political route later on.

Soon after the chief justice came to his position, Jeffersonian Republican and Federalist politicians were warring against one another concerning congressional reorganization of the judiciary and the use of Marshall's judicial review in the *Marbury* case (1803). It has been the prevailing view up to the present that he turned the Court around from a weak, nearly insignificant institution to a position of great importance. At first, Clay agreed with Jefferson that the new order was destructive, but he came to admire Marshall's approach to law. This was in spite of Clay's bitter confrontations with the chief justice's relatives in Kentucky, such as his brother-in-law Humphrey Marshall, to the point of dueling with him. And a number of other relatives, particularly land claimants, were opponents against Clay's clients. Yet there was a subsequent philosophical linkage between the two, Clay the lawyer and Marshall the judge, in political and economic terms.[4]

Among other justices, the learned Joseph Story was quite important. The New Englander also served a long time, a decade after Marshall's death. In addition to his work in court, he was a pioneering professor in the Harvard law school. Though a Jeffersonian Republican and an appointee by President James Madison, he became an arch conservative in politics, squaring with Clay's Whig program. In his later days he seemed isolated, as President Andrew Jackson created a majority by his appointees on the bench. It became a Democratic tribunal where poor Story was neutralized. Clay, too, was unhappy about the Court's new composition.[5]

Though Marshall had presided over a tribunal of cooperative colleagues until his death in 1835, one of them, William Johnson, had dissented frequently. His opinions could suit some of his Jeffersonian friends but tended to be obscurely expressed, even to the point of creating doubt whether he concurred or dissented with the decision. Anyway, he was an interesting person and a desirable member of the Court.

Clay had a degree of influence when it came to identifying the appointment of justices. When a vacancy arose for a member who would also travel on the federal circuit in Kentucky, he got the appointment of Robert Trimble by President John Quincy

Adams. Trimble was known to support Clay's current effort for state bankruptcy legislation whereas Thomas Todd, who died at this juncture, had disagreed on constitutional grounds. Filling the vacancy with Trimble would tip the Court favorably on this question of state bankruptcy power for his client Ogden, Clay believed. Though he got the appointment of Trimble, Clay still lost some points in the pending case before the Supreme Court on this subject in *Ogden v Saunders* (1827).

As an outgoing secretary of state, Clay tried again for another appointment two years later when Trimble died. He pressed President Adams to appoint a good friend, John Crittenden, another Kentuckian. Clay asked Marshall to help persuade Adams to do so. But Marshall refused because he thought it was improper to intervene. "It has the appearance of assuming more than I am willing to assume," he answered, even though he obviously had a high opinion of Crittenden's qualifications. "Were I myself to designate the successor to Mr. Trimble, I do not know the man I could prefer to him," he wrote. Did Clay show Marshall's note to the President? At any rate, it was impossible to get Senate approval because Jackson had been elected president, and his followers wanted to wait during the interim until the Jacksonians in Congress could confirm a Democratic justice.[6]

The Court's work changed very much during the first half of the nineteenth century both in character and volume. The population of the country increased from five to twenty-three million persons. In settled territory, it extended from thirteen original eastern states to a frontier beginning to reach the Far West. Its economic growth mounted as industrialization and urbanization developed spectacularly, concurrent with a dramatic flow of settlement of vast transmontane lands. These trends obviously affected operations and expansion of government at all levels, including state and national legislatures and courts. With only a modest supply of resources and time the Supreme Court had much to do in these years. One must remember that the justices considered protracted arguments, decided many novel questions, and handed down intricate decisions in premodern conditions. They had no clerks, nothing but quills and ink for writing in their own hands. They listened hour after hour to loquacious arguments of counsel, afterward reading what written briefs they might get in very compact form, if any, exchanging views in free-flowing, informal conferences back at their boarding house, composing their opinions tediously and often reading them orally in the dim light of the Capitol basement. Then they might set out to ride circuit along rugged roads and perilous river channels to remote, lower federal courts. How different from modern procedure!

The Supreme Court had a full docket of cases through this period. It is well known today that the Court heard an increasing number of cases on constitutional law, but it had many more nonconstitutional ones—791 of them during the years 1816 to 1835, compared to only 66 constitutional cases. They came in because the parties were citizens of different states or because the questions involved laws of the United States. The cases were authorized by congressional legislation.[7]

Subjects in these twenty years mainly concerned contracts and real property questions. Marshall and Clay were well informed in those areas. The trend by the 1830s was away from numerous early maritime issues, which had not interested Clay, who argued only one case of that sort in the Court.[8]

The effects of economic change in the country upon the work of the justices are apparent. One subject was the important development of corporations, legally as well as commercially. Their standing as parties in the court strengthened steadily by a line of decisions, one of which was the *Dartmouth College* case (1819), over the next thirty years. Significant questions coming into the Court involved many banking corporations, as in *Osborn* (1824)—the case establishing the Court's jurisdiction to decide cases brought against state officials by the national bank, incorporated by Congress. *Osborn* showed the way toward increased judicial business.

Clay acquired his professional expertise in the West where land was a leading economic interest. In these cases he often had to reconcile old feudal rules with changing circumstances in a modern setting. This was a slow process, which now appears to have tilted toward antiquated law too often in the hands of the chief justice, no doubt reflecting his strong personal involvement in land grants and speculation. In *Johnson v Pannel* (1817), for example, he upheld a poorly described claim to land, supported only by "common intelligence." Here he seemed to rely not only upon ancient authority but sympathy for the claimant.[9]

American jurisprudence drew upon the current concept of republicanism, aiming to protect the people against dangerous governmental power and social privilege by an emphasis upon the popular basis of government and society. In this conception, remnants of the old order must give way to a different legal system infused by republican principles. Republicanism, premised upon the ethical purity of citizens as well as officials, was a widely held ideology in the nation during the early nineteenth century. Marshall's court was affected by this ideology, though some of its decisions shielding vested rights and governmental powers posed a counter force.[10] Furthermore, an earlier variant of republican ideology, called classical republicanism, accepted differences of citizens' status produced by economic conditions, looking very much like social classes. It was a trait illustrated in the law practice of the future Jacksonian president, Martin Van Buren, as shown in a recent biography. The lawyer-politician worked for a long while against valuable holdings of old manors by proprietary grants in New York. He obtained a legislative revocation of some but not all of the original privileges of landlords on the ground of defective provisions extended by the assembly. Here was a modification of what could have been a broader decision.[11]

Republicanism was a familiar term in politics as well as law. It was a contrast to earlier American colonial conditions, which had been imposed by British imperial control. Jeffersonians now used it to describe their party as Republican in the 1790s and beyond. In this sense, Clay subscribed to it. From the time he was a youngster in Chancellor Wythe's office in Virginia, he saw and admired Jefferson, Madison, and other Republican leaders of that party, the adherents of states' rights. John Breckinridge and other young men with similar backgrounds were of the same mind. When talking about politics, Clay often declared his constitutional views had been clearly laid out in the Virginia and Kentucky states' rights resolutions of 1798 against the alien and sedition laws. He continued to say so on later occasions when his comments had some inconsistencies.

Clay was not unique in his flexible positions, for the very idea of republicanism was flexible too. He became the chief advocate of an American system for governmental impetus to economic growth by protective tariffs, internal improvements, and national banks. In this combination, there was a mix of Jeffersonian and Hamiltonian thought. Clay's model of desirable policies sought to accommodate both practical needs and ideology.[12]

Abraham Lincoln in his legal and political career from the 1830s into the Civil War years helped define the character of republicanism. As a Clay Whig, he joined the movement for an economic basis of national policy, which he believed necessary for progress. As a lawyer, he represented railroad interests, which he believed were contributing to that end. And more to the point, he was a founder of the Republican party, applying republican principles to prevent the expansion of slavery. Midway in the war for the Union, he voiced a view of the American republic that has gone down in history as a central theme. Among other contributions was his Gettysburg address, defining the republican credo. His statesmanship rested not only upon politics but upon legal institutions, which he understood well.[13]

Thus, although an analysis of republicanism is helpful as a guide for understanding early American legal history, it does not lend itself to uniform conclusions. It was used by different persons with different interests and behavior, even to defend the institution of slavery before the Civil War.[14] In truth, it was quite unstable. Unquestionably, it was an elusive ideology then and remains so now. Nevertheless, it does provide a cautious view of past thought and conduct.[15]

Another interpretive theme in explaining legal development

has been the rise of a market economy during the early nineteenth century. It involved industrialization and the acceleration of commercial growth. These tendencies often undermined the idea of classical republicanism by weakening the importance of social status and emphasizing dynamic roles of property and the bargaining power of individuals in a competitive setting. Still, there was a strong demand for tariffs to protect industry, though contrary pressure for free trade as well. Financially, state and national systems of banking also created issues of vigorous controversy. All these were the subjects of Clay's involvement in both politics and law.[16]

During the early years of Clay's practice, he was involved in important changes of both procedures and substance in law. Rules for judicial admission of evidence were sometimes unclear or inadequate, allowing arbitrary decisions and miscarriage of justice. Lawyers often drew upon English treatises and reports, such as the widely used manual of Chitty. The result, however, could be mistakes in the intricate process of pleading. As a young member of the state legislature, Clay contributed to an improved code for the courts to follow. There was also a problem with the procedure at equity which long ago in England had been a liberal option to the common law but had grown too hidebound and therefore needed improvement. Clay observed the persistent confusion about when and how to use equity in an important case up from Louisiana near the close of his lengthy career.[17] He himself faced serious procedural difficulty in criminal law, too, where judges often mishandled the admission of evidence and instructions to juries. True enough, he benefitted from these deficiencies when he could range widely in defending clients, especially by resorting to his eloquence at trial. But criminal cases were not an important part of his practice.

In addition to these involvements in strengthening the legal system, Clay served on the Senate Judiciary Committee. In that role he secured passage of a measure to add another Supreme Court justice, who was assigned also to the federal circuit court in Kentucky. The latter assignment greatly relieved the impossible burden upon the existing United States district judge. Others had tried to do something about the problem but had failed. Then there was Clay's service for a time as a professor of law at Transylvania University in Lexington. Altogether, his professional credentials were quite good.

The question whether to adopt or reject the common law persisted, even though congressional judiciary laws recognized it in defining the scope of federal jurisdiction. And lawyers, including Clay, had studied English and American common-law treatises in preparation for their careers and did cite them despite continuing criticism that the common law was not consistent with the republican character of America.

A thorough study by Nelson of the "Americanization" of the common law in Massachusetts shows that it consistently supported economic growth. Thus it pushed aside an earlier emphasis of religious elements in the state's courts and favored creditors more than debtors as time passed.[18] Even if religion had been more influential in New England than in other jurisdictions, it is still clear that everywhere the economic impact was much the same. Common law remained a significant factor in the country's legal systems. Undoubtedly, this was true in Clay's Kentucky and in other states in the West. Another example from New England was the *Dartmouth College* case (1819). In arguing it in the Supreme Court, Webster relied heavily upon the English common law rule of charitable trusts in defining the legal status of this educational corporation. Chief Justice Marshall's opinion was very influential in constitutional history, drawing as it did from counsel's argument. In general, this precedent from the extensive list of Webster's cases illustrates the broad acceptance of the common law in the United States. It was typical of a trend in the young nation.

Some exceptions remained. In Louisiana for a time civil law survived into midcentury. One of Clay's important cases in the Supreme Court was *Livingston v Story* (1837), involving his opponent in Jacksonian politics, Edward Livingston.[19] It turned on the question of applying the civil code, which interestingly

Livingston had helped establish in Louisiana. But Clay argued for relying upon it, while Livingston's attorney also interestingly called for invoking the common law. Clay lost, illustrating the trend toward the common law throughout the country. Still, Clay felt comfortable about retaining the civil law in its period of decline. Often he had cases in New Orleans, where some of his relatives and close friends lived. There was a similar trend involving Spanish law in Florida and Missouri, ending in a general preference for the common law despite some mingling of cultural backgrounds.

From the beginning of his practice, Clay emphasized land as his particular specialty. His choice of focus was natural since he began his legal career where land was so important. It was a powerful dynamic in the new state's economy, and here was a great opportunity to get ahead, as Clay's rapid successes demonstrated. In the Blue Grass a young lawyer could easily attract clients to acquire land titles and collect handsome fees, often in the form of land.

But there were complications challenging the attorney. One was the horrid tangle of titles. Much of the desirable tracts had been registered or otherwise claimed in Virginia before Kentucky's detachment from the Old Dominion. Now laws and records in the two commonwealths were incompatible or very unclear. Clay's cases demonstrate this situation. There was also the fact that Kentucky's procedures were utterly inadequate. Boundaries of land were not well identified. Rivers and creeks, trees, and fuzzy memories of settlers, all made for legal dispute. Added to this situation was the inexpert, if not corrupt recording of sales and titles in the capitol at Frankfort, allowing mistakes and fraud. It was credibly said that Kentucky was a lawyer's paradise to collect fees from land cases.

A complication arose in handling land cases from Ohio where, years earlier, Virginia had granted many tracts to veteran soldiers of the American Revolution; some of these tracts were claimed also by Kentuckians. Another complication could be the condition of multiple ownership of property, based upon a form of joint tenancy with purchasers sharing title and able to use or sell their portions of the land. An optional pattern was so-called tenancy in common, which allowed individual rights to market parts of tracts, free of other tenants. It was preferred by speculators rather than residents and was a widespread procedure in Kentucky.

Though borrowing from English practice, American features of land law were not as restrictive, encouraging development and permitting transfer and individual control instead of retaining old barriers. Nevertheless, Clay's federal cases in the Marshall era revealed the tendency of the chief justice and that of others such as Justice Story, a tendency to hold on to ancient rules of the common law, sometimes to feudal institutions such as proprietary privileges. If Marshall innovated to an extent in formulating new legal doctrines, he was surprisingly rigid on this subject. The Supreme Court, speaking through one of his fellow justices, reflected this orientation in Clay's case of *Green v Biddle* (1824). It was the lawyer's most important effort on a land question, though a very disappointing failure.

Overall, Kentucky did encourage marketing by easy requirements of title and transfer. Its policies often favored the actual occupant of land, it seemed, rather than claimants relying upon dubious public records. This was true of the doctrine of adverse possession by a settler for a period with little, if any, formal proof. Land would be an important and accessible medium of progress in this economy.[20]

So this was the setting in which Clay the lawyer would practice in the half century after his arrival from the East. With a good introduction to the law over several years in Virginia, he had followed the westward path of many others to the new state of Kentucky. Its growing, promising society encouraged prospects of the young man of twenty-one, likely to attain a prominent standing in politics as well as law. Both features of his career would develop favorably and interact with one another, much as they did in the case of his friends and associates. It was a season of mobility for him and his contemporaries.

His personal character was, of course, an important asset in the career he was now beginning. Then and throughout his many years as a lawyer-politician, he would project energy and magnetism. Some would say he could be overbearing, indeed egotistical. Yet he drew upon these traits to become a bold, often constructive figure, whether in the practice of law or in the politics of a half century. In history he is better known as a partisan leader, unceasingly seeking election to the presidency, which meant he sought his individual advancement more than contributions to the public good. Even if true, was he much different from adversaries like Andrew Jackson or party colleagues like Daniel Webster?

As a lawyer, he would project traits similar to those of a politician. It was common then much more than now to carry on an active legal practice while holding public office. Obviously there could be desirable effects at a time when institutions of the republic were taking shape and could benefit from this connection. But that obviously depended upon the ability and performance of those combining these dual roles. Could Clay do so?

It would not take long for him to show he could. He soon gained an understanding of public affairs and the legal system by attending meetings of a debating society in Lexington, not only listening carefully but explaining his views. He could attract wide notice and approval in this fashion. His skill in speaking was a decided asset, either in the courtroom or a political gathering. Without restraint, he explained merits and defects in state and national constitutions, as when he advocated the gradual emancipation of slaves. The impact was attractive as well as instructive. His delivery was crisp and very moving.

2

EARLY PRACTICE

Clay was a native Virginian, the son of a church minister in Hanover County a few miles north of Richmond. His father died when Henry was four, and his mother soon remarried. As a child, he received scanty instruction from a rural schoolmaster when not performing tasks required on a farm. Carrying bags of grain on horseback to market along paths cleared in a forest, he acquired the nickname of Millboy of the Slashes. In later years, his image was often that of a statesman's ascent from humble origins to national fame. But that was not entirely accurate. His mother owned substantial property, and his stepfather Henry Watkins was a person of some means. Nevertheless, in 1791, when Henry was fourteen, the Watkinses decided to move westward to Kentucky, as so many in their region were doing. His parents felt it best to leave him in Richmond for work and hopefully a better education.[1]

At first, the lad was employed in one of the town's stores, but before departure his stepfather had arranged with the clerk of the state court of chancery to take him on as an assistant. By this route, young Clay gained favorable notice of George Wythe, well-known chancellor of this court. Wythe, now seventy, had a distinguished reputation as a signer of the Declaration of Independence, learned professor of classics and law at nearby William and Mary College, and teacher of many public figures, including Thomas Jefferson and John Marshall.

Clay served as a secretary, taking dictation from the chancellor, crippled by arthritis. Another major chore was to copy and file documents. Wythe was impressed by his intelligence and winning manner. True enough, judicial and academic demands upon Wythe's time did not allow as much legal instruction as Clay would have liked or needed. Yet he fared decidedly better than most apprentices—indeed, better than he himself, contemporaries, and biographers would later portray.

For one thing, the wider scene was conducive to getting ahead. In and around the state capitol he saw fascinating, gifted persons: Secretary of State Jefferson, Congressman James Madison (both intimate friends of Wythe), Chief Judge Edmund Pendleton of the Virginia high court, future Supreme Court justice Bushrod Washington, and John Marshall who would skillfully head that tribunal. There were also promising youths, such as Littleton Tazewell, Walter Jones, and Thomas Ritchie, all stimulating friends. One vehicle for both intellectual growth and social enjoyment was the debating society, which sharpened valuable oratorical talents of aspiring lawyers and politicians. Another outlet, of course, was the crowded barroom.

He spent his final year of study with one of Virginia's leading lawyers, Robert Brooke, a former governor and currently state attorney general. Brooke could open a practicing lawyer's perspective and was more accessible because Clay lived with the Brooke family. His close relations with them lasted for many years, especially with a younger brother, Francis Brooke, whom he found very compatible.[2]

On November 6, 1797, at age twenty, he appeared before the three members of the state's court of appeals, produced a certificate of preparation from Robert Brooke, and after what was probably routine procedure received a license to practice in the Old Dominion's courts.[3] Within the month he set out for

Kentucky, joining the tide of migration to this former western county of Virginia, now a bustling state in the Union. He arrived at the town of Lexington in the center of the bluegrass, which was already claiming the character of another American Athens. In spring 1798, just before his twenty-first birthday, Henry Clay obtained his license to practice in Lexington's Fayette County Court, with subsequent certification in other locations—all automatic recognitions of his license back in Richmond, it seems.[4]

The tall, thin newcomer's ready wit and mobile expressions attracted attention at once. He had a bold, charming style. Very sociable, he could drink whiskey, swear, and gamble with the best of a circle of young men in this western town. Already he had learned how to use his resource of eloquent speech with great effect. And he was not hesitant in moving center stage in the political arena, whether to urge amending the state constitution to emancipate slaves[5] or to join fellow Jeffersonian Republicans in condemning the Federalist administration in Washington. His fellow lawyers seemed quite compatible: George Bibb, a future chief justice of Kentucky; John Breckinridge, soon to become a member of Jefferson's cabinet; Robert Wickliffe, one of a family long active in politics; and especially James Brown, also a former student of Wythe but a few years older than Clay.

Brown became Clay's brother-in-law. They married two daughters of Thomas Hart, a leading merchant-manufacturer who had come to Kentucky in its early stage of growth and had gained a sizeable fortune. Brown would remain in Lexington for a few years before moving to New Orleans. Clay stayed and obviously benefitted socially and professionally from his connection with the Harts. He and eighteen-year-old Lucretia were married in April 1799 and soon built a house next to the Harts and across Mill Street from his law office.[6]

Without delay he was attracting business on what seems to have been a rather litigious scene. Much of it came before the county court in Lexington, but some of it in the capital at Frankfort and in similar county courts throughout the state. These tribunals had a general jurisdiction, including civil and criminal suits, and they employed procedures of both law and equity by a traveling state judge and two local laymen with uneven or no expertise. Then the lawyer carried some cases to Kentucky's Court of Appeals, whose proceedings were reported in published volumes annually. Beyond that layer was one of the several national circuit courts in the country, composed of only an overworked judge from the United States District Court in Kentucky. In addition to district cases, that person had also to conduct the kinds of circuit business that in older states was handled by a traveling federal Supreme Court justice. There was deep dissatisfaction with this uneven feature of the judiciary in the new West, and Clay would try to get reform.[7]

Much of his practice involved collecting debts owed to eastern merchants. For a while this was one of Clay's chief sources of income. He received a percentage (5 percent or more) of what he collected either by getting a court's judgment or by warning he might file suit to seize property. His mercantile clients, creditors in Philadelphia, Pittsburgh, Baltimore, and other places, were themselves hard-pressed as the economy tightened due to a sharp decline of foreign trade during the European war at the turn of the century. And the financial condition of their western customers was anything but liquid.[8]

One can understand Clay's situation by looking at his close connection for more than a decade with a prominent merchant of Baltimore, William Taylor. Their active correspondence shows he made an active well-organized effort to shake delinquent debtors into payment. His personal attention to detail impressed Taylor, who responded with his thanks.[9] Where Clay encountered special trouble was finding satisfactory ways of forwarding receipts he collected. A persistent difficulty was getting enough acceptable bank notes and other media. He resorted not only to bills of exchange but to promissory notes, to several kinds of paper, even to agricultural produce. Would the merchant accept cordage, an available Kentucky product, he asked?[10] Then another vexation was the unreliability of the mail, due to stealth or mishandling in transit. Perhaps he ought to use the familiar technique of cutting notes in half and sending them on at different times, he thought.[11]

Anyway, his compensation from this client was gratifying: it totaled over $7,000 through the years 1800 to 1803, and more came later. This fee was not excessive, Clay argued when Taylor complained, for the rate was customary and freely stipulated. Clay was always alive to what remuneration he could get as a lawyer.[12]

Important as early questions of debt were, those about land were far more important in the long run of Clay's career. Land law became the specialty in which he could claim unusual expertise over a period of fifty years. One reason he moved in that direction was the great economic significance of land to westerners especially. In Kentucky after Clay's arrival, land was certainly a powerful dynamic both to hardy settlers and to aggressive entrepreneurs. But there were difficult legal problems because Kentucky had not become a state until 1792, and there were earlier grants of the same locations from Virginia. Furthermore, the Old Dominion had previously ceded an area north of the Ohio River to the United States as a temporary national territory which became subject to a congressional land ordinance. Applied to many other parts of the union, this ordinance of 1785 had established a policy of rectangular survey prior to sale and allowed fewer disputes and less litigation about boundaries there. In Kentucky, however, transactions of registry and later transfer of title were about as uncertain as anyone could imagine. Deeds described tracts as bordered by particular trees as well as forks and branches of creeks, often identified by squatter settlers or local lore. These were the confusing conditions the lawyer faced.[13]

An early piece of business consisted of assisting his father-in-law Thomas Hart in drawing up a deed for property, valued at six hundred pounds. It was only the start of recurrent work he performed for Hart and family.[14] That the young man had already gained the confidence of clients is illustrated by the power of attorney given him by a Virginian to convey as he saw fit.

An even better sign of his reputation was the trust displayed by John Breckinridge, the prominent Jeffersonian Republican senator, when leaving for Washington. He turned over a number of pending cases to Clay, nearly all concerning sizeable amounts of land. Though Clay attended to preparation and hearings of these land disputes over a four-year period, he got judgments in only three. The others were settled out of court, dropped, or dismissed.[15]

An interesting retainer involved a large acreage along the Licking River, requiring protracted work and promising a handsome bonus for victory. A group of claimants included Thomas Bodley, clerk of the Fayette County Court, and Thomas Marshall, who had surveyed an extensive area of early Kentucky and was the father of the Supreme Court chief justice. Clay entered an agreement with adversaries of this group and was promised twenty pounds for every thousand acres he might recover against Marshall and a sizeable payment from recoveries against Marshall's associates. The well-known agrarian philosopher, John Taylor, also sought his help in a shaky claim to some of this land. Clay lost the decisions because they rested upon the date of actual settlement by the other side instead of the date his clients had only entered title.[16]

He fared no better against the Marshall interests when he carried a land case to the Supreme Court in 1807, his first appearance there. Opposing counsel was Humphrey Marshall, brother-in-law and cousin of the chief justice and currently Clay's bitter adversary in Kentucky politics as leader of the Federalists. In fact, Humphrey's wife was also recorded as a party to the controversy, since her father, Thomas Marshall, had entered title to this tract, too. At issue was a very large area along Green River, a typical grant by Virginia before Kentucky statehood, described in terms of a river branch and trees with marks no longer visible. Clay contended that such a description was too vague and furthermore that the question was merely one of fact, not of law, therefore ineligible for appeal to this court. Despite that persuasive point, John Marshall's colleague on the bench, Justice William Johnson, delivered an opinion that these vaguely worded cessions would have to be interpreted loosely. At least the location of Green River was indisputable, he jauntily observed. Much land litigation related to military warrants awarded to veterans of the Revolutionary War. Were they superior to claims based only upon settlement? Clay made one of his numerous arguments on this problem in *Hickman v Boffman* (1808) in the state court of appeals where he represented a person holding such a warrant. Despite defendant's reliance upon prior settlement a long while earlier, as confirmed by the county court, Clay successfully contended that a military warrant on federal authority must prevail. As he put it, a military warrant was "of a higher dignity in law" than local certificates of settlement alone.[17]

In the future he liked to tell the story that after beginning practice with no money, he had hoped to earn a hundred pounds the first year, but that he surpassed that goal decidedly.[18] Considering his legal education, his social connections, including his favorable marriage into the Hart family, and especially his ability and energy in specializing in these land-title cases, one has to conclude his sizeable financial returns were no surprise.

His pattern in taking a case was to ask for compensation with a portion of the land involved in it, and often the amount depended upon the outcome. By such an agreement with Alexander Black he received 1050 acres along the Licking River. He got a fourth of a tract he recovered in a suit for Thomas Donnell and the same in another for Michael Stoner. His correspondence reflects many similar arrangements.[19]

As a result, within a few years he held a great deal of property. His tax bill for 1808 listed about ten thousand acres, fourteen slaves, and forty horses.[20] In addition, he acquired numerous town lots and buildings, one of them a hotel in Lexington. He erected his comfortable Mill Street residence and a neighboring law office.[21] Soon he acquired an estate, known as Ashland, south of town and started a dignified dwelling there. No wonder his brother-in-law James Brown wrote: "On all hands it seems agreed by such of your countrymen as visit us [in New Orleans] that you are at the head of your profession, and are rapidly growing rich—Indeed some accounts assure us that you are acquiring money 'as fast as you can count it.' All that I infer from this is that you are *doing extremely well* for I have long been sensible that the public rumors respecting purses of lawyers were, like most other reports, subject to great exaggeration."[22]

Clay was very impressive before a jury. Six-feet tall and thin, he moved gracefully about the courtroom. He was a striking figure, holding the complete attention of spectators. His voice traveled from a slow, subdued delivery that connected him to his audience, and then he advanced his case, with his low key alternating with sharp emphasis. At first organlike, his tone deeply affected everyone present. Nearing the close, he punctuated his conclusion with great spirit. And more often than not, he got his verdict. Some people compared him to Patrick Henry, who was also a native Virginian. In truth, Clay's silver-smooth diction as well as emotional impact did resemble that of the great Revolutionary patriot.

He did not take as many criminal cases as those in other branches of law. He was adequately prepared but not a specialist in this area of jurisprudence. Still, he was a formidable trial lawyer because of his attractive style and moving eloquence, enabling him to give sway to interesting innovations. Information on these cases is not as full as those on questions of property, which were more likely to be appealed and reported in published volumes. One thing is clear: he seldom lost a criminal case.

A sensational trial involved Doshey Phelps, who became so irritated in a domestic quarrel with her sister-in-law that she shot her dead. It appeared to be an obvious murder, but Clay got a verdict of temporary insanity—he called it a "delirium"—which made the act punishable as manslaughter and allowed a penalty of only a few years of imprisonment. This lenient disposition of the case may have been due as much to the husband's forgiving his wife, the killer of his sister, as to Clay's argument.[23]

A similar instance was the murder trial of a man and his son, whom people in Lexington called "the two Germans." Here, too, there was no doubt the defendants had killed the victim. Clay again obtained a lesser verdict of manslaughter, followed up with a plea for an arrest of judgment, discharging the prisoner. The lawyer could often win popular sympathy for his clients, in this instance probably helped along by the presence of a distraught wife and mother in the courtroom. She overwhelmed him with gratitude after adjournment.[24]

Perhaps the most incredible outcome of a murder trial, again with Clay for the defense, concerned a certain Willis. Though the evidence was strong, the jury had divided, causing a new trial. Now Clay contended that this amounted to inflicting double jeopardy on the prisoner, whereupon the judge told him he could not assume that ground. Very irritated, the attorney refused to continue the case and walked out, which seemed to rattle the judge into sending him a message, now allowing the argument. The jury was quite affected by these strange proceedings and came out with a verdict of not guilty. Clay had indulged in questionable reasoning on double jeopardy, the judge had been unjustified in cutting him off so abruptly, and the jury was altogether distracted. At any rate, Willis was free. His conduct does not seem to have improved, and Clay recognized it when he met the young man on the street one day, boasting of his good fortune. According to an early account, he said, "Here comes Mr. Clay, who saved my life." Clay countered, "Ah Willis, poor fellow, I fear I have saved too many like you who ought to be hanged."[25]

Old sources claim that Clay never lost a capital case, but a modern historian disagrees. One of his defendants, Henry Field, was convicted of killing his wife and was hanged. Later his slave confessed to the deed. The slave's confession may have been forced, but this exception to Clay's supposed perfect record had a sad outcome for poor Field.[26]

In a rare instance when he served as a prosecutor, in the trial of a slave who was hanged for killing a brutal overseer, he gained a conviction. Clay had argued that a slave must humbly endure even such a severe correction. Looking back on the circumstances, he told a friend he regretted the execution "more than any other act of his professional career."[27]

In this period Clay generated wide visibility as a lawyer by defending Aaron Burr in one of the nation's best-known criminal cases. He participated only in the early stage of proceedings that would move from a lower court in Kentucky to a spectacular treason trial, heard by Chief Justice Marshall in the East. As a political as well as legal question, the prosecution of this gifted but highly controversial figure began a long-standing debate about what Burr had actually done and how he ought to have been treated at law.[28]

Grandson of the famous minister Jonathan Edwards, veteran officer of the Revolutionary army, consummate New York politician, and Republican vice president, Burr had killed Alexander Hamilton in a duel and had been effectively neutralized at the capital by his rival, President Jefferson, and other party leaders. After leaving office in spring 1805, Burr set out for the West in search of some enterprise to recoup his former prominence. Proceeding down the Ohio and Mississippi, he encountered an enthusiastic welcome wherever he stopped. Clay in Lexington, William Henry Harrison in Cincinnati, Andrew Jackson in Nashville, governors, senators, and other notables reflected these warm popular feelings. On a privately owned island in the river off Marietta, Ohio, a well-to-do Irish immigrant, Harman Blennerhassett, was enchanted by the great man and soon began a project of helping him with money, recruits, boats, and guns, all to support American colonization in Louisiana along the disputed border of Spanish Texas, it was said. This so-called Bastrop grant would be useful to territorial expansionists, should war with Spain break out. Would that also verify the periodic hint of western secession from the Union? The person who might assure success of the scheme was the unprincipled governor of the Louisiana Territory, the commanding general of the army there, James Wilkinson, with whom Burr was in frequent contact.[29]

During the next summer of 1806, Burr returned to the West

to move ahead on some plan or other. Exactly what, was unclear. In Kentucky, Burr's critics, mostly confirmed Federalists, did not doubt his intention: it was, they declared, to lead an unpatriotic, treasonable secession of the transmontane states, linked to subjugation of Spanish territory as the future realm of this egocentric filibuster.

Such was the view of Joseph Hamilton Daveiss (he assumed the middle name in memory of Burr's victim, the party's saint). A Federalist appointee as United States district attorney for Kentucky, who was another brother-in-law of John Marshall and an associate of Clay's inveterate opponent Humphrey Marshall, Daveiss smelled a rat. As soon as Burr arrived in 1805, the attorney had begun to send President Jefferson long, alarmed letters, warning that Burr in league with General Wilkinson was conspiring to detach the western states from the Union. Spain would continue to supply funds to Wilkinson, he predicted, as it had to other subversives. Without reserve, Daveiss suspected more persons linked to some such plan: Senators John Breckinridge and John Adair of Kentucky, John Smith of Ohio, General William Henry Harrison, even Clay. Months passed from January 1806 onward without any acknowledgment from Jefferson, who, Daveiss felt, was uncooperative in taking action against this peril because the chief executive and he were of different party persuasions.[30] At last, he resorted to the United States Circuit Court, whose presiding judge, Harry Innes, was another person Daveiss had mentioned as a malefactor. That Innes belonged to this network seemed to him authenticated by a close friendship with Clay.

Now the district attorney moved ahead without Jefferson's approval. In early November 1806, he presented a motion to Judge Innes for the apprehension of Burr, to be questioned for violating an American law prohibiting civilian attacks upon a foreign country with whom this nation was at peace. He carefully avoided charging Burr with treason, a constitutionally defined act of war by Americans against the United States, for that would have been more difficult to prove.[31] Predictably, the judge preferred to move more slowly and ruled he did not have the power to require Burr to submit to questioning without prior action by a grand jury. Though Burr did so appear on his own volition, Innes still insisted upon a grand-jury finding, which Daveiss could not get because a key witness, Senator John Adair, was not available. For the time being the district attorney was checked. Clay visited the courtroom in Frankfort during these proceedings, then joined a crowd on the street celebrating the outcome.[32]

Daveiss returned to the task the first week in December 1806 by again filing a motion before Innes for a grand jury. Now he would face Clay as one of the defense counsel. Burr had urgently requested this representation because he enjoyed Clay's declared sympathy for him as a sufferer of political persecution. But the lawyer hesitated. One complication was his temporary appointment to fill out a term in the Senate in Washington, to which Burr, knowledgeable about congressional business, answered that Congress would not transact any important business until the new year. So there was no hurry to get to the capital.[33] The other point causing Clay's pause was a need for Burr's absolute assurance that he was innocent of these charges. Right off, he got a written answer. Burr had no design to separate the western states from the Union, he wrote. Furthermore, "I do not own a musket nor a bayonet, nor any article of military stores, nor does any person for me, by my authority or with my knowledge." He concluded by declaring he had explained his plans to "the principal officers of the government, and I believe are well understood by the administration [headed by Jefferson] and seen by it with complacency. They are such as every man must approve."[34] A stretch of the truth, but it was enough to obtain Clay's agreement to take the case.

At a second hearing in early December, Clay emphasized his belief in Burr's innocence. As defense counsel, he assured the court he "cared not in what attitude he should be considered as standing; but he would instantly renounce Col. Burr and his cause, did he entertain the slightest idea of his guilt, as to the charges exhibited against him by Mr. Daveiss." And to affirm his principled representation of the controversial defendant, he refused any compensation from Burr. In extravagant phrases Clay declared, "You have heard of inquisitions in Europe, you have heard of the screws and tortures made use of in the dens of despotism, to extort confession; of the dark conclaves and caucuses for the purpose of twisting some incoherent expression into evidence of guilt. Is not the project of the attorney for the United States, a similar object of the error?"[35]

A heated exchange between Clay and Daveiss occurred when the district attorney offered to assist the grand jury in examining witnesses. Clay complained that this altogether novel procedure would transform the grand jury into a trial jury at the expense of justice. Judge Innes ruled against the request, but surprisingly Burr himself consented to a presentation of written questions for possible use by the panel.[36] The only significance of this dispute was to feed animosity between the opposing lawyers in the days ahead. Still, it was an interesting issue of defendants' rights.[37]

Among several others, Kentucky's ex-Senator John Adair, a crony of General Wilkinson, finally appeared before the panel but with no evidence to cause it to indict. The prosecutor was especially disappointed when the editors of the Frankfort *Western World,* which had been sounding the alarm against Burr for a long while, reneged by saying they had no firsthand knowledge of illegal acts. So the grand jury decided it had no true bill, much to Clay's satisfaction. Public opinion in Frankfort seemed to share that feeling, reflected by enthusiastic applause around the capitol and a gala ball that evening.[38]

Such was not the view of President Jefferson in Washington. During the hearings in Kentucky he had received reports he thought incriminated Burr. The principal allegation came from Wilkinson, till now Burr's collaborator, who produced Burr's coded letters, outlining a plan to attack Spanish Mexico and to seize New Orleans as a base. Though this would be a misdemeanor, a violation of federal law, and might indicate constitutionally treasonable behavior as well, the authenticity of the documents Wilkinson produced was questionable. Certainly he was a slippery informant and, in fact, he had doctored the text.[39] Nevertheless, hostile to Burr as Jefferson was, the chief executive believed what he read. Forthwith, he circulated a proclamation to the country, warning of serious danger and stopping movement of Burr's men and equipment down the Mississippi.[40]

The proclamation came out on November 27, 1806, between the two hearings in Kentucky. Clay did not know about it then or before he set out for Washington to attend the Senate. When he arrived, he called upon the president, who showed him the Wilkinson papers. Jefferson had no doubt that Burr intended to invade Spanish provinces and detach western states as parts of a grand empire. The young senator immediately changed his mind about Burr's plans, entirely illegal in his opinion. "We have been much mistaken about Burr," he concluded. "When I left Kentucky, I believed him both an innocent and persecuted man." On the contrary, he said, Burr "had formed the no less daring projects than to reduce New Orleans, subjugate Mexico, and divide the Union."[41] Thereafter, Clay never changed his mind about this episode. Why he reversed his views so completely is difficult to understand. One can believe that his strong attachment to Jefferson and the Republican party had much to do with it.

Whatever Burr hoped to accomplish now collapsed. Wilkinson had decided he preferred to retain his subsidy from Spain instead of cooperating with Burr. This meant he would not incite a border conflict, upon which his former partner's operation had depended. And the general's exaggerated warnings fueled excessive official reactions. At Blennerhassett's island a small band of Burr's followers fled down the river, as militia from the neighborhood occupied and plundered their camp. This episode provided authorities a questionable justification to charge Burr with levying war against the United States, that is to say, procuring treasonous conduct of about twenty untrained recruits. Burr himself was arrested in Louisiana, then escorted overland to Richmond for trial in the federal circuit court, Chief Justice Marshall presiding.

Through summer 1807 prosecutors pressed the case ardently,

while Jefferson supervised strategy by his letters from Washington, which displayed partisan animosity against the defendant. At the trial, Marshall's rulings turned out to be a detailed formulation of the law of treason. He emphasized a strict constitutional definition of treason as actually levying war against the United States by an assembled force. If that were proven, then a person procuring the treason from a distance would also be guilty. But Burr's counsel could prevail in successfully contending that the few men on Blennerhassett's island were merely making their way peacefully to a projected colony in the Bastrop tract. That may well have been the option that their leader had in mind, lacking action along the Spanish borderland by the United States army that Wilkinson had promised and then abandoned. Following the chief justice's instructions on the law, the jury found Burr not guilty on the facts.

Clay was unpersuaded. Though thinking Burr innocent when he had served as defense counsel, he now firmly believed him guilty and meriting punishment. He said so when Attorney General Caesar Rodney asked him to prosecute Burr in an Ohio misdemeanor case, involving the charge of illegal plans to invade Spanish territory. He declined to represent either side with the excuse he did not have the time to do so. Besides, he thought taking the assignment would leave the impression that he was using information he had gained from Burr when he had represented him in the Kentucky hearing.[42] Nevertheless, he had concluded Burr was guilty.

Clay did feel sympathy for Harman Blennerhassett, who suffered even after escaping a treason conviction. The Irishman had contributed extensive financial support of the operation for recruits, boats, and other supplies. Burr's wealthy son-in-law Joseph Alston had provided more. Much of their contributions consisted of lending their credit to Burr by endorsing his bills. Alas, he played the scoundrel by overcommitting this resource, misrepresenting its use, finally absconding to Europe, showing personal traits for which he was notorious. Poor Blennerhassett ended up in debtors' prison for a time. In the months after the

Richmond treason trial ended, Blennerhassett retained Clay to help him handle claims of creditors, who eventually took over the Ohio River island estate, his slaves, and other property.[43] It was a bitter experience for this gullible admirer of Aaron Burr.

The first phase of Clay's legal practice, which had begun with admission to the Kentucky bar, ended in 1811 when he became heavily involved in national politics. He then had to turn over most of his business to his friend Robert Wickliffe, who offered to handle some suits without remuneration but did accept large fees from a number of pending cases.[44]

Looking back, one can see that Clay had now built a reputation as a very active, effective lawyer. For example, a random selection of thirty of his cases in the Fayette County Court in a four-year period showed he lost only one.[45] His specialties had been debt collections and land disputes, both concerning important economic interests of that part of the country, about which Clay was well informed. A lesser involvement was criminal law where his learning was minimal, but his eloquence and style gained him huge success.

Contemporaries viewed Clay's professional ability more positively than historians often have. His clients and associates could point to his large financial gains in land-title litigation as proof of his mastery of that field. The general public was much affected by his eloquence and persuasive reasoning in a courtroom. Judges and other attorneys might have some reservations, however, about his depth if an issue required argument drawing upon complex doctrines of jurisprudence. Some biographers have so portrayed him.[46] Clay himself contributed to that view by often expressing his regret in not applying himself more seriously to the study of law in his early years. Actually, his preparation under Wythe and Brooke, as well as his contacts with gifted persons of bar and bench in Richmond, placed him well above average for his day.

At any rate, the forums in which he practiced often did not demand sophisticated presentations. The county courts of Kentucky were each composed of a hard-pressed circuit judge and two lay judges, who could be influenced by emphasis upon simple common-law principles, even just common sense, more than high-level legal discourse. A study of reports of state appellate and federal Supreme Court cases indicates it was also true there.

Nevertheless, Clay had a respectable proficiency in general fields of law. Soon after arrival in Lexington he was appointed professor of law and politics at Transylvania University, a post he held for a few years. Other academic and professional relations with the institution continued a long while. He served as a trustee, taking an interest in its affairs, one of which was its involvement in recurrent litigation about the university's claims to land, granted by Virginia for its establishment before Kentucky statehood.[47]

After 1804, as a member of the state legislature, he made a determined effort to get a new federal district court for the three states of Kentucky, Tennessee, and Ohio. He pushed through a resolution to ask representatives and senators in Congress to press for that reform of a system in which western states lacked adequate access to circuit tribunals. The overworked district judge in each of the three states had also to hear circuit cases. Then when Clay went to Washington to serve as a senator in 1807, he became a member of the Judiciary Committee and drafted a bill for change. It passed Congress as proposed. A new seventh circuit was created, with an added United States Supreme Court justice who would also preside over cases in it by travel to each state and receive help from the district judges. The young senator justly took pride in this legislation.[48]

Clay contributed also to improvements of Kentucky's legal institutions. He was much involved in reforming the structure of the county courts, to which he traveled regularly during the period of primitive roads and inns, thus drawing from that arduous experience. He helped revise the state's criminal code, perhaps involving less of his own expertise.[49] But he did not approve a movement then underway across the country to prohibit citations to English common-law cases and commentaries after American independence in 1776. In fact, in an argument before the appellate court he sought to defy a new state law providing that prohibition, but was overruled.[50]

On one legal subject he made no progress and displayed an alarmist feeling, derived from the nation's politics. He shared with fellow Jeffersonian Republicans a dissatisfaction with the increasingly nationalistic decisions of Federalist Supreme Court justices. The development of judicial review in *Marbury v Madison* (1803) and other cases disturbed him. He urged adoption of a constitutional amendment "limiting the powers of the F[e]deral Judiciary to the enforcement of the laws of the U[nited] States." This would forbid jurisdiction over questions about the dividing line between state and national powers. He spiritedly remarked that "unless the amendment contemplated does take place, a dissolution of the union must be the ultimate consequence. Two independent Judiciaries, neither acknowledging the superiority of the other, may for a time subsist without inconvenience, but in the end they will come into collision, and the concussion which they will produce must destroy one or the other government." Years later, how differently he would see the problem of federalism, of dividing state and national powers during controversies about states' rights, the Union, and the Constitution.[51]

In a legal career from his admission to the Kentucky bar as a young arrival from Virginia in 1797 in the bustling western town of Lexington until he left for the congressional session of 1811 in Washington, Clay had gained a very favorable professional reputation. To be sure, this was not surprising in light of his good fortune to study under the tutelage of Chancellor Wythe and the experienced state Attorney General Robert Brooke back in Richmond. His natural gifts of keen intellect and striking personality had also prepared him for decided success as a lawyer. Income from ample fees soon made him a person of extensive means. Added to this was his early reputation as one of the state's ablest politicians, a familiar asset for a successful law practice in those days. Within a short time, he had gained a position of leadership of the state's Jeffersonian Republican party.

A specialty at this stage was collection of debts in the West, drawing him into profitable relations with merchants in eastern cities. It was then a well-known pattern across the country for young attorneys, such as Clay in Kentucky and Daniel Webster in New Hampshire, to handle this kind of business.

Frequent clients were free-wheeling speculators or other claimants for broad areas of western lands. An example was the batch of cases involving the interests of Chief Justice Marshall's relatives. Clay lost some of this litigation, including those he appealed to the Supreme Court during his first appearance there. Often he was handsomely rewarded—in many instances he worked on a contingent basis, paid with large pieces of land or other property if he gained a favorable decision. He encountered quite complicated questions of titles because of careless policies of Virginia in its wholesale grants of tracts in Kentucky before detaching it as a new state. Though the well-known case of *Green v Biddle* (1823) in the Supreme Court had broader constitutional implications, it arose out of these tangled circumstances.

Clay's extensive practice as a lawyer in land cases would provide him with a useful base for long involvement with national land policies as a politician. Through the Jacksonian period of the 1820s into the forties, he was a leading figure in discussing important subjects such as preemption rights for settlers in the public domain, which he opposed, and distribution of federal revenue to the states from land sales as a fund for internal improvements, which he advocated tirelessly. He spoke about these issues with assurance.

He did take a few criminal cases, though with some reliance upon his oratory and personal effectiveness to sway juries or to influence judges to hand down less severe rulings than prosecutors reasonably expected. In defending clients charged with murder he saved the lives of a good number and got them off with verdicts of innocence or manslaughter instead of the death penalty, which the facts and the law seemed to command.

Undoubtedly, his most controversial criminal case was his defense of Aaron Burr, accused of treason. It addressed the question of how to define that crime more specifically than the Constitution's language, which referred to waging war and leading an assembly of force against the United States. Though Clay was not involved in the judicial hearing before Marshall's federal circuit court in Virginia which decided the case, he was involved earlier before the circuit court in Kentucky. Burr was then wandering about in the West, stirring suspicion that he was organizing an armed secession from the Union.

In the first part of this story, Clay had joined many Republicans in an enthusiastic welcome of a prominent figure in their party. So it was no surprise that he rejected any notion that Burr was intending to disrupt the Union in a military operation. Not only sharing a widespread sentiment favorable to the former vice president, as a lawyer Clay unhesitatingly agreed to represent Burr before the federal circuit court in Frankfort. He ought to have recalled Burr's slippery past before accommodating him. Nevertheless, he conducted Burr's defense with ability. The opposing counsel was every bit as politically biased against Burr as Clay was for him. Anyway, Clay did argue on good grounds against the district attorney's arbitrary strategy in questioning witnesses before the grand jury. As a lawyer, he handled himself well, though later historians have not paid much attention to this preliminary chapter in their accounts of Burr's "conspiracy."

3

⌒⌒

ECONOMIC ISSUES

For ten years during and after the War of 1812 while Clay directed his attention to political affairs, his law practice was inactive. Then in the early twenties he encountered worrisome financial trouble, partly involving his endorsements on defaulted notes of friends and relatives. Like many lawyer-politicians of the day, he went into court in search of a better income from fees. Until he became President John Quincy Adams's secretary of state (1825–29), he carried on a brisk business in cases reflecting governmental economic policies, notably on land and banking.

Although the postwar years were a time of optimism, of nationalism and expansion in some respects, there was an opposing current of localism, of disturbing maladjustments. People in the West blamed a spreading depression upon banking abuses, an unbalanced foreign commerce, and exploitation by eastern interests. Opinion about remedies varied widely. In Kentucky, for example, the branches of the newly chartered Bank of the United States had supposedly inflicted hardship on farmers and merchants. Debtors in growing numbers sought relief at the state capital by legislative moratoria on their obligations. Critics often pointed to lawyers for their legal manipulations and especially to the Supreme Court for its sweeping exercise of judicial review, frequently nourishing national power at the states' expense.[1]

One of Clay's cases arising out of these conditions was *Green v Biddle* (1823). It originated in Kentucky's effort to protect settlers on land claimed by Virginians. Many of these claimants had obtained warrants granted by the Old Dominion before detachment of Kentucky as a new state in 1792. It was an unrestrained, wholesale process in which a buyer could sometimes get a hundred acres for two dollars. The location was uncertain, bounded by trees and creeks, plotted on rudimentary sketches or none at all. It was clear many of the claims had not been perfected by settlement or sale by the grantees. And worst of all, the tracts were often occupied by Kentuckians, who might have no recorded title at the land office in Frankfort.[2]

To protect these occupants from aggressive claimants, the state legislature sought to ensure their past investment of labor and capital if they were evicted. In 1797 it enacted one of a series of laws, providing that claimants had to compensate occupants for their improvements and could not collect any retroactive rent from them. Another measure in 1812 stipulated that these improvements need not have been valuable or permanent. In administering the policy, Kentucky judges inclined to rule for occupants generously. Such laws as these were being adopted elsewhere in the country. They departed from English common law, which had classified all unauthorized improvements as "waste" not eligible for compensation.[3]

The key element in a mounting controversy was a "compact," stipulated by Virginia and accepted by Kentucky in 1789 before gaining statehood: "All private rights and interests of land within the said district [Kentucky], derived from the laws of Virginia prior to such separation, shall remain valid and secure under the laws of the proposed State, and shall be determined by the laws now existing in this State."[4]

Disagreement of the two states intensified in early 1821 when heirs of a Virginia claimant, John Green, filed suit in the federal circuit court against a Kentuckian, Richard Biddle, at least nominally in possession of a piece of land and therefore having standing as an occupant.[5] Probably, the real opponents were prominent speculators and developers on both sides. For example, the Marshall families were quite interested in the outcome.[6] The two circuit judges divided in opinion on the questions, and an appeal went to the Supreme Court in Washington on the issue of constitutionality of the occupant laws at its term that winter. A decision there favored Green of Virginia, but as an amicus curiae, Clay came into the chamber and successfully moved for a rehearing because Biddle of Kentucky had not had counsel for argument of the case.[7]

In Frankfort the legislature took another step to vindicate the state's position. In December 1821 it appointed Clay and George Bibb commissioners to go to Richmond and obtain a negotiated settlement. Upon their arrival there a few weeks later, Clay addressed the legislature with a defense of Kentucky's policy and with proposals for an agreement. It was an eloquent speech with moving recollections of a fond native son, confident of Virginia's sense of justice. He cited early instances in which Virginia itself adopted the same sort of regulations protecting improvements as those presently in question. He proposed two options to end the dispute: accept Kentucky's very fair measures requiring claimants to compensate ousted occupants for their improvements of the land, or establish a bilateral commission to determine a solution. In fact, he contended, the compact of 1789, on which Virginia now asserted its rights, had called for such a commission. This clause might forestall the Supreme Court's deciding the case.[8]

In March 1822 Virginia rejected both of Clay's options on the ground that the dispute had to be decided by a judicial body instead of his version of a commission. No wonder, because it appeared the Supreme Court would uphold Virginia's position again. It heard reargument of *Green* by counsel (including Clay) but postponed a decision until next term.[9]

Still hoping to prevail, Clay got the Kentucky legislature to authorize him to work with an appointee from Virginia to set guidelines for a board of six neutral judges who would make binding decisions. First, these rules had to be approved by the two legislatures. In June he and Benjamin Watkins Leigh, his counterpart and reliable friend, completed their plan. It provided that the board decide the validity of unlocated land warrants. The state of Virginia must guarantee that it would indemnify Kentucky if any of its individual claimants failed to comply with rulings by the board against them. Kentucky predictably approved the guidelines in November 1822.

Not so, Virginia. Its rejection, however, was a very close call. The lower chamber of representatives approved, and then the senate disapproved by the thinnest margin. Clay was extremely upset by its opposition to the convention's provision that Virginia guarantee payments by stubborn claimants. When asked if he would withdraw this provision, he spiritedly answered that a guarantee of compliance with the board's rulings was essential. Why enter an agreement yet reserve the power to withdraw if disappointed in the outcome?[10] Nevertheless, though he regretted the result of the "business between our respective states," he would not "dwell upon it, especially as it has probably terminated finally, and had therefore better be forgotten as soon as it can be."[11]

Clay's only hope for success, slim though it was, now depended upon reargument of the *Green* case, which he immediately undertook. He had to combat somehow the postponed but adverse opinion of 1821 a year earlier by Justice Joseph Story, who had said it was unanimous with six of the seven justices "present." That seems to have been a misleading comment, for in both hearings Chief Justice Marshall did not record a vote, no doubt because his relatives had a large interest in Kentucky lands.[12] Furthermore, William Johnson would soon make it clear he did not agree with Story. And Thomas Todd of Kentucky, though also silent, would not disapprove his state's policy. So no more than four or perhaps three instead of six among the seven judges could be counted upon to approve Virginia's position. Still, Clay himself could not be confident of recruiting a majority of four for Kentucky. Much depended upon which way the absent Bushrod Washington would go after this second hearing.

Story's opinion in the first hearing had chiefly rested on his application of a common-law principle that rights and titles to land must be determined by the state making the grant, Virginia in this instance. Surprisingly, he had not even mentioned the contract clause of the Constitution, which prohibits states from impairing the obligation of contracts (article 1, section 10). Perhaps he uncharacteristically did not because Virginia's counsel had not. Both they and Story did refer to the compact of 1789 between the two states, providing for a bilateral commission to settle disputes, but did not point out that no commission had sat. Story had concluded that the Kentucky laws were unconstitutional, the question submitted by the two divided judges of the lower court; yet he did not identify what part of the Constitution supplied his authority.[13]

During reargument in March 1822, Clay's opponents did not make these mistakes, for they did cite the contract clause as the constitutional basis in their case. Thus the compact of 1789 was a contract to which the two states were parties, one of whom (Kentucky) had impaired its obligation.[14]

Clay replied that the compact itself was an unconstitutional restraint on Kentucky's power to govern its internal affairs, a states' rights position quite familiar then and in the future. He also contended that since the Constitution (article 1, section 9) required congressional approval of interstate pacts and since the national legislature had not done so specifically in the law admitting Kentucky to the Union, Virginia's reservation on controlling land warrants in the compact was inoperative. He repelled the assertion that Congress had implicitly approved that provision when it admitted Kentucky. But his best point charged Virginia itself with not observing the compact of 1789, since it had not joined Kentucky in establishing a commission to find an amicable compromise. He had in mind, of course, the action of the Virginia legislature opposing the procedures he himself had put forward in the negotiations.

Until now the contract clause had been invoked in this court to protect only private parties against a state. Yet Clay did not attack the legal novelty of interpreting it as a restraint upon an agreement between two states. That dimension would subsequently be seen as the most significant innovation of the case and would have been a better target for Clay to attack in *Green*.[15]

Now he moved to a philosophical plea: "This Court is not a mere court of justice applying ordinary laws. It is a political tribunal, and may look to political considerations and consequences. If there be doubt, ought the settled policy of a State, and its rules of property, to be disturbed? . . . The [Kentucky] laws now in question are founded upon the great laws of nature, which secure the right resulting from occupation and bodily labour. The laws of society are but modifications of that superior law. . . . Surely this Court will respect those rules of property which had their origin in early colonial times, which were adopted by the parent State and have been so long acquiesced in and confirmed by inveterate habit and usage among the people where they prevail."[16]

Clay's argument was strong when he emphasized the failure of Virginia to approve a commission of the two states to determine a fair solution of this dispute, as provided in the Constitution. Yet he did not react vigorously enough to Virginia counsel's reliance upon the contract clause, for that new dimension deserved a more credible explanation by justices and lawyers than it received. And the Kentuckian's position was even weaker when he emphasized an extensive sovereign power of Kentucky to thwart federal intervention of this sort. He was reflecting angry opinion prevalent back home in the style of a vocal states' righter, and seemed inconsistent with his well-known nationalism. Furthermore, his appeal to natural law as a restraint upon a state was a gloss upon the Constitution, which can be found nowhere in that document. Yet in this period, judges and lawyers often drew upon this philosophical principle of a higher law to affect decision making.

A year after this second argument, on February 27, 1823, the court announced its decision. Justice Bushrod Washington, who had been absent at the first hearing, delivered a long opinion invalidating the Kentucky occupant-land law. Again there was a weak attempt to show a judicial solidarity. But of the seven justices, Marshall, Todd, and Brockholst Livingston did not participate; and Johnson produced a separate opinion, which apparently was concurring but really dissenting. The effect was to reveal the court deciding a novel and important constitutional question by a three-to-one division, lacking a majority of the whole bench of seven.

Washington reiterated Story's previous discussion of common-law principles which, he ruled, supported Virginia's policy. Then he rejected Clay's view that Congress had never approved a specific provision for an interstate commission on land disputes and therefore had not approved the terms of the compact of 1789 about claimants in general. On the contrary, the justice believed that Congress had implicitly sanctioned that procedure when it passed the law as a whole admitting Kentucky as a state.

Unlike Story and unlike Clay, Washington paid attention to the contract clause, prohibiting state impairment of obligations. He could draw upon the reasoning of Virginia's counsel but not upon any prior interpretation by this court of these few words of the Constitution to settle the present issue. Whether justified or not, the result was to open intensive debate about the soundness and the desirability of the Supreme Court's disposition of *Green v Biddle*.[17]

Criticism began with Justice Johnson's strange opinion. He was quite dissatisfied with Washington's position, which, he believed, dangerously impinged upon state power. Though he would not uphold the claim of Clay's client, Biddle, he would return the case to the lower court which first tried it. And he would leave such questions to a state tribunal since the subject matter required it. The problem with his wanderings was that the case had come up on a division of two federal circuit, not state, judges who had certified they could not agree, and they probably would not have agreed if the case had been "returned" to them. Contrary to intimations from Story and Washington, Johnson certainly did not fully concur with others for a unanimous disposition of the issues, not to mention those who were silent.[18]

Kentucky strongly complained about the judicial blow. In his message to the legislature, Governor John Adair attacked the court for wrongly favoring Virginia, which had refused to settle the controversy amicably before a neutral commission, as provided in the compact of 1789. And a minority of the justices, he said, had erroneously applied that document as a contract between two states in constitutional terms to invalidate the occupant laws. What would follow? Would the national government employ its superior force to implement the decision? If it did, he darkly predicted, there would be "an event of all others to be deprecated."[19]

An aroused legislature adopted firm resolutions, addressed to Congress. To avoid "the degradation and oppression" of the court's opinion, they called for a guarantee of "coequal sovereignty with the STATES which compose this union." Even Humphrey Marshall, the veteran Federalist member of that body and Chief Justice John Marshall's brother-in-law, voted for these resolutions, probably because of the impact of the case upon his own extensive land holdings.[20]

Despite understandable dissatisfaction with the decision in *Green,* Clay urged the governor and legislators to avoid extreme reaction. He had a "warm conversation" with Governor Adair, whose message he called "ill advised." He predicted nothing more extravagant from the legislature than a few intemperate paragraphs in its resolutions. "The mouth and the pen are happy conductors to let off bad humors. Not that I do not really think that we have much justly to complain of in respect to the fate of our occupying claimant laws. But then I do not think that we ought to make any Civil War about them."[21]

One feature of the case, which Clay as well as many others thought especially objectionable, was the three-to-one division of justices. On such an important question as this, he believed a majority of the whole court of seven was essential.[22] Occasionally, his dissatisfaction led him to severe comment, such as his remark that the justices were "superannuated."[23]

More often, he aimed his criticism at Virginia. He emphasized its present inconsistency with its frequent skirmishes over judicial review at the expense of its sovereignty. Earlier, that state had emphatically disagreed with the Supreme Court's assertion of jurisdiction superior to that of its tribunals in the *Cohens* case concerning constitutionality of a congressional lottery law. But when Virginia wanted help on the land-occupancy question, it welcomed federal intervention.[24]

Despite his dissatisfaction with the court's handling of the present problem, Clay maintained his belief that judicial review was a necessary institution to uphold national authority in face of extreme states' rights. As he had once expressed it and still believed, if a choice had to be made between state separation from the Union and consolidation of power, he would go for consolidation. As much as he disapproved Kentucky's debtor-relief policies of that time, he said, "We feel in this State the want very much [of a negative] decision of the Supreme Court on our execution [relief] laws. We must hobble on as well as we can until the next term."[25] Unlike many critics then complaining about judicial activism, he welcomed it on other questions.

Clay's perspective on the court's role in government and on the *Green* case in particular can be understood by looking at congressional debates at this juncture. In both chambers controversy grew, as decisions invalidating state legislation were handed down. In this context Story's opinion at the first *Green* hearing in 1821 prompted Senator Richard Johnson of Kentucky to an attack. To counter such judicial pronouncements as this, Johnson pressed for a constitutional amendment to give the Senate appellate jurisdiction about the validity of state laws.[26] So much for the principle of separation of powers. In later sessions of 1823–25, Clay resumed his seat in the House and participated in discussions of possible reforms. One would require a quorum of the court's seven members or a certain number of them to decide constitutional cases. On other questions the chief justice or all members would have to file written opinions.

Robert Letcher, a colleague in the House from Kentucky, proposed that at least five of the seven must join in constitutional decisions. Clay advocated this version. He shared some objections, expressed on the floor, to the direction the court had recently taken and emphasized a faulty, dangerous image it had acquired. Do not glorify these jurists, he warned: they were only human with less than perfect virtue and intellect. How persuasive his argument was is unclear.[27] At any rate, no reforms were adopted, not even one for a badly needed expansion of the circuit court system.

In Kentucky, *Green* had little practical effect upon occupants of land claimed according to its ruling. A general determination to resist such claims seems to have been quite effective. Besides, branches of the state government blocked the claims. Soon after the Supreme Court's decision the legislature passed a law forbidding claimants from selling occupants' land and requiring them to carry out improvements within a year or forfeit it.[28] The Kentucky Court of Appeals took a large step further in a decision holding that *Green* was not a binding constitutional interpretation because it was affirmed by only three of seven justices, a minority of the court.[29] Whether or not this tribunal's reasoning was correct, it was another barrier against enforcement of the judicial pronouncement.

Green as a restraint on Kentucky's land policy finally expired in the Supreme Court. *Hawkins v Barney* (1831) applied the state's statute of limitations in order to protect occupants who had possessed land for seven years without claims against them. It was prima facie proof of claimant consent, said Justice Johnson, the dissenter in *Green,* who appropriately delivered the majority opinion.[30]

In looking back upon this complicated case, one can venture a few generalizations. First, an obvious difficulty the characters in the story faced was the chaotic condition of land policies of the two states. Absent an accurate system of survey and record keeping, there was bound to be the kind of trouble that developed. Conflicting claims in great number would arise as the push of the frontier and the lucrative business of development made it difficult to devise a fair policy.

Second, when the *Green* case went to the Supreme Court, the members did not have their finest hour. There were absences and abstentions aplenty, handicapping their honors in coming up with a decision of high quality and credibility. Furthermore, the role of Justice Story, despite his notable learning, was no exception. He declared the Kentucky occupancy laws unconstitutional without identifying what constitutional provision applied. His reliance on common law was somewhat better, but that would not be a reason specified in the Constitution for his opinion after the first hearing. When there were only four of the seven members of the court actually participating in the decision, with one of these being Johnson, who really dissented, he based an important precedent on a division of only three to one. This would inflame reaction to the outcome.

Third, Justice Washington's opinion after the second hearing, based on the contract clause of the Constitution, was faulty. Not only an unprecedented interpretation of the clause, it was inapplicable to the facts. Undoubtedly, the framers had not intended the clause to apply to a contract between two states as parties.[31] Aside from whether he should have used the questionable original-intent standard of interpretation, the circumstances of Kentucky's detachment from Virginia would have been more appropriately classed a compact than a contract. The Constitution does refer to an interstate compact,[32] but there were also problems with that kind of relationship. Congress had not then or ever explicitly approved the clause in the so-called compact of 1789 between the two states about land warrants, as required in the Constitution. Nor can one believe that the legislators did so implicitly when they adopted the law admitting Kentucky as a state. Modern studies of this topic indicate that after *Green* the constitutional compact clause, as distinguished from the contract clause, was invariably used in interstate relations. Yet even these authors do not convincingly identify the Virginia-Kentucky agreement as a compact.[33]

If it was a compact, then why did Virginia refuse to activate a joint board of commissioners to arrive at a mutually satisfactory, just settlement? Indeed, that is what the agreement of the two states had provided. At any rate, that would have been a far better precedent for future problems than the *Green* formula.[34]

Technically, the case was probably a fictitious suit involving two parties with no genuine adversarial interests, as constitutionally required. Green had title from Virginia to land in Kentucky, but Biddle had only weakly alleged a real settlement of the land in dispute. Nevertheless, many cases that that tribunal has heard and decided over the years have been fictitious.

As for Clay's role in this litigation, it seems contrary to his longtime interest in land policy. At this point he argued in behalf of many squatters, occupying land without establishing a valid title. Yet in future congressional debates Clay would vigorously oppose a lenient national system of preemption on public lands. Politics and a lawyer's work were not always consistent.

In this period there were other important cases involving the contract clause and the economy that Clay argued before the Supreme Court. A prominent one was *Ogden v Saunders* (1824–27), defining the constitutional limits of state bankruptcy laws, though it had even broader implications over the next century.

The question arose in New York where George Ogden of that state had assigned a bill of exchange to Lewis Saunders formerly of Kentucky, then living in Louisiana. Ogden fell into financial trouble, did not pay Saunders on the bill, and filed for bankruptcy under a New York statute.[35] The critical feature of the transaction became the relative dates of Ogden's bill and this law. The impact of the state measure of 1801 upon the debt to Saunders in 1806 had been prospective and therefore posed an undecided constitutional issue. If the effect of the statute upon the debt had been retrospective, it would have been invalid under a recent precedent. To complicate the circumstances, Saunders of Louisiana had sued the New Yorker in a federal court, generating an interstate controversy. He prevailed there, and Ogden's heirs appealed to the Supreme Court.

Clay and two others were counsel for the appellants in a three-day hearing of *Ogden v Saunders* in March 1824. Lawyers for the other side included Daniel Webster and Henry Wheaton (who was also the official reporter of the Court). In urging the justices to uphold the state bankruptcy law, Clay and his associates had to distinguish the present case from *Sturges v Crowninshield* (1819), which had held that a state bankruptcy law had unconstitutionally impaired the obligation of a prior contract and had left the question of future contracts undecided.[36] Therefore his task was to maintain state power to regulate this future contract while his opponents would deny power over both kinds of legislation, retrospective or prospective. Clay wished very much to provide state relief to debtors by filling the void due to the lack of national bankruptcy legislation, a situation he had been seeking to change in Congress.[37] As an advocate of positive federal power generally, his lawyer's brief for this active state policy might appear inconsistent. The same might be said of a possible inconsistency with his current disapproval of Kentucky's controversial debtor-relief program. But he was expressing his belief that a sound debtor policy of individual states, in the absence of one for the whole country, was necessary for economic growth.

As expected, he confronted strong positions of Webster and Wheaton, counsel on the other side. They contended that the Constitution conferred upon Congress the power to enact not only "uniform," but also exclusive national laws on bankruptcy. So states had no such authority, whether the legislation was prospective or retrospective in relation to the date of a contract. Indeed, they went further to insist the obligation of a contract was derived from the universal laws of nature, immune from shifting experiments with positive laws of states. No doubt with Chief Justice Marshall in mind, they emphasized the financial disorder of the Confederation era when delinquent debtors got unfair help from states. That was the condition that produced the Constitution's contract clause, they declared.[38]

In behalf of New York's law, Clay advanced even further than necessary to contend that a state had full power, concurrent with Congress, to enact either prospective or retrospective bankruptcy statutes. Thus the word "uniform" did not mean exclusive of state law. On a practical level, he warned, "If the Court should pronounce the State bankrupt codes invalid, and Congress should refuse to supply their place by the establishment of uniform laws throughout the Union, the country would present the extraordinary spectacle of a great commercial nation, without laws on the subject of bankruptcy."[39] Webster, who was also working in Congress for national action, was not as pessimistic.

Several arguments by counsel moved into a theoretical zone by defining the word "obligation" in the contract clause. As Clay saw it, an obligation was created when a person entered a contract, subject to state laws. The obligation became part of a particular contract. On the other hand, Webster connected the obligation to a superior natural law, immune from political vagaries.[40] If that were true, however, government would be incapable of exercising indispensable oversight, Clay reasoned.

The case was continued from 1824 over the next three years to add arguments on the interstate dimension due to diversity of state citizenship of the two parties. Did the law of one state unconstitutionally conflict with a law of another state? Since he was occupied with duties as secretary of state, Clay did not participate in the second hearing.

At last, in a four-to-three division Justice Washington delivered the majority opinion. He compromised his belief in an exclusive national power by upholding the New York law according to the time of its application to an agreement. While he preserved the *Sturges* precedent, prohibiting state bankruptcy intervention on past contracts, he approved such legislation against future contracts. In so narrowing the scope of the contract clause, the court broadened state jurisdiction over the important subject of debtor relief, as Clay had wished.[41]

Then in a separate consideration of the question of whether the New York law could restrain Saunders, an out-of-state citizen, Justice Washington again spoke for the majority of four to say no. He could cite as precedent only *McMillan v McNeill* (1819), which had glanced at the issue in unclear language, though it seemed to disapprove an interstate reach of the contract clause. Justice William Johnson filed a strong opinion, agreeing there could be no extension of a state's power beyond its own boundaries.[42] So the present decision of *Ogden* in 1827 was not a restatement of settled doctrine but a pragmatic accommodation of constitutional law to a developing national economy, less hindered by local barriers.

Clay the lawyer lost his case for Ogden's heirs, who relied on the invalid New York measure. It could not protect them from Saunders of Louisiana. The question of the validity of the New York measure could have been decided on that point alone. Clay the politician, however, obtained a ruling on bankruptcy fitting into his economic nationalism, reducing the scope of individual state policies which he had just propounded as a lawyer. Still, in his view, it remained for Congress to enact legislation to energize the power the Court had awarded that body.

Marshall was not happy to be in a minority of three of the seven members. Indeed it would be the only occasion during his many years as chief justice when he did not carry his associates with him on an important constitutional case. In an aroused opinion, he budged not at all in his conviction that the contract clause forbade any state impairment of a contractual obligation, retrospectively or prospectively. He clung to his position that an obligation derived from the law of nature, universal principles, not state legislation. It then inhered in the contract for its entirety. Typically, he worried about the peril of reverting to the financial chaos among the states in Confederation days.[43]

In analyzing the *Ogden* case, it is relevant to recognize the need for some rules to assure justice to both creditors and debtors. The Court provided a durable formula. Limiting the range of debtor relief to prospective, not retrospective legislation seems to have been the right and fair approach. If a debtor entered a contract when a bankruptcy law was in place, he could know the character of his obligation without risk of new conditions imposed by legislation. The other element of the *Ogden* decision was the prohibition of one state's law extending to that of another state, a rule essential to a nationalizing economy. Even knowledgeable scholars have not given adequate weight to that point.

But then and later, a general disapproval of any interference with fulfillment of financial obligations existed, so that adopting an appropriate policy on bankruptcy was very difficult. It was grounded on belief that release from debts was to condone violation of moral principles. Understanding that viewpoint helps explain why the country limped through the nineteenth century without effective bankruptcy laws, particularly national but to an extent state enactments as well.[44]

The standard history of debtor relief shows that New York actually paid little attention to the Supreme Court's adverse pronouncements. Indeed, for years, that state continued the same procedure for bankruptcy as it had previously. And there were few judicial cases there concerning the contract clause and insolvent debtors.[45]

Clay himself did not change his mind about the desirability of some form of relief to desperate debtors. Years later, in 1840 during a severe depression, he sponsored a bill in the Senate for that purpose. And at the next session he exploited a Whig victory in the presidential election to pass a national bankruptcy law. In the course of urging this policy, he insisted it was undoubtedly constitutional, despite much misunderstanding about its specific shape. It is interesting to note he did not comment on his own connection with the *Ogden* case.

His success in getting his bill through Congress depended on complicated logrolling with other legislation, so that the statute did not survive a devastating warfare between Clay's Whigs and

President John Tyler's states' rights followers. It was repealed in 1842. This was another proof that the nation was not ready to establish a national system.[46] In the short time the law lasted, a large number of bankruptcy proceedings were initiated and their disposition remained the basis of much litigation for a long while. Clay was counsel in some of these lingering cases. One was *Houston v Bank of New Orleans* (1848), in which the Supreme Court upheld a broad coverage of the law for his client.[47]

In considering the long-range importance of *Ogden*, one can see that a basic concept of Marshall's minority opinion in relation to the contract clause survived. In the late nineteenth century stockholders sued their corporations to get judicial rulings against rate structures imposed by state regulations. They contended that the lowered rates were depriving them of their financial interest, property in dividends, without due process of law, prohibited by the Fourteenth Amendment of the Constitution. Their legal actions also rested on their contractual relations to corporations as stockholders. They could and often did succeed in court by getting decrees when the laws were either prospective or retrospective. The impact was the same whether by substantive due process of law or by a remodeled contract clause. Both were invoked to resist state regulation of corporations. Prospective legislation affecting business could be weakened not only by reference to state charters but also to the contract clause, shielding stockholders as well as company officers, who sometimes generated what amounted to collusive suits.[48] Marshall would have approved the effects, if not this strategy. It amounted to a prospective application of the contract clause, supposedly forbidden by *Ogden*.

During the 1820s, Clay had been involved in two significant cases, *Green* and *Ogden*, concerning interpretation of the contract clause. He made an extraordinary effort to protect a land policy of Kentucky in *Green* when he sought a rejection of the first opinion by Story against his state's occupant-claimant law. Virginia had opposed Kentucky's measure and relied upon the compact protecting land titles it had issued when detaching the new western state. Clay represented the interest of occupants who had shaky titles or none at all and were threatened by Virginia claimants. In addition to his losing argument in court for a correction of the adverse pending decision of 1821, he worked hard to get an agreement by Virginia to submit the dispute to a bilateral commission. Despite his persuasive advocacy of that approach, he failed to get Virginia's consent to these proposals. And he failed also in his reargument to change Story's pending opinion. Furthermore, he was irritated by the surprising novelty of considering the constitutional contract clause as a restraint upon states as parties to a contract. To his credit, he urged Kentucky politicians to control, though not abandon, their fiery objections to the outcome of this case. And today his formula of a calm legal solution, relying on the constitutional provision for peaceful and negotiated interstate compacts, seems correct.

In *Ogden* he was not completely successful in upholding the validity of state bankruptcy laws. He managed to get only a partial decision saving their prospective if not retrospective effects. Through the nineteenth century attempts in Congress to establish a uniform and comprehensive national policy failed except for occasional and brief periods. This left the matter to whatever states could or would do. And that was even less after adoption of the due process clause after the Civil War, which was also a formidable barrier to state power. These problems indicated the desirability of obtaining a national bankruptcy system. The case showed the importance of an often underemphasized second part of *Ogden,* prohibiting state bankruptcy legislation from application to interstate situations. Clay's tireless effort in behalf of his American System promoting the country's economic development seemed all the more justified.

4

BANKING

While much involved in the contract-clause cases of *Green* and *Ogden* during the early 1820s, Clay gave more attention to legal business for the Bank of the United States (BUS). His motive was still to recover from his worrisome financial situation, including a large indebtedness to that institution. He had mortgaged his residence and land at Ashland for $40,000, as well as the Kentucky Hotel in Lexington for $22,000—obligations not wholly retired until 1830.[1]

In June 1820 he put an announcement in the *Kentucky Reporter:* "I intend to recommence the practice of the Law, and for this purpose I shall attend the Court of Appeals, the Circuit Court of the United States at Frankfort, the Circuit Court of the U. States at Columbus in Ohio, and the Fayette Circuit Court."[2] That winter he gave up his post as speaker of the House and refused reelection as a member, effective in March 1821. Already he had assumed the position of superintendent of the bank's legal affairs in Kentucky and Ohio.[3]

He had also settled the question of his fees in an exchange with the BUS president, Langdon Cheves. Pointing out the heavy load of litigation, about four hundred cases in the two states and debts of $2,000,000, he suggested an annual fee of $5,000. Cheves consulted the board of directors and offered $3,000, with additional compensation when he appeared in court as the solicitor for cases that arose in Kentucky. Surprisingly, Clay replied he was quite satisfied.[4]

An early, protracted problem involved a large debt to the bank by Senator Richard Johnson and his brother James. Altogether, the notes amounted to $130,000, secured by lands and town tracts in Kentucky and Ohio. Clay was reluctant to accept Johnson's offer to turn over the property, for he was then advising the bank to avoid acquiring real estate. Besides, he was uneasy to move against a friend and such a prominent figure. Consider Johnson's public services and "the esteem in which he is everywhere held," the lawyer advised. Eventually, he conceded the need to settle the debts by a complete transfer of the brothers' holdings.[5]

As he began work in collecting debts to the bank, Clay inclined toward a lenient strategy. Recognizing the dreadful impact of hard times across the country, the desperate condition of those unable to meet their obligations, he advised the board back in Philadelphia to take a deliberate approach. It might require as much as five years to eliminate the enormous debts now in default. Meanwhile, he warned, do not gain the reputation of a heartless money changer, oppressing farmers and merchants of the West.[6]

Nevertheless, with the bank's approval, he set about forming a system that became increasingly efficient and strict. As legal superintendent for Kentucky and Ohio, he monitored the cashiers at BUS branches in Lexington, Louisville, and Chillicothe, as well as the agency in the Cincinnati office, which for the time being had lost its status as a branch equal to the others. At locations in Ohio, lawyers, called solicitors, handled cases in court while Clay himself acted as solicitor in Kentucky. In addition, there were clerks who kept records on proceedings in litigation and their financial aspects.

As months passed, he developed close oversight of personnel

and procedures by frequent correspondence from Lexington or by travel to the Ohio offices. He insisted upon prompt, effective work in the courts to get judicial executions on debts. And he improved methods of record keeping on the subsequent status of compliance.[7] He tightened enforcement by placing notice in the newspapers to debtors, though he was not required to do so. He rationalized that it was "further evidence of that spirit of forbearance and moderation, which has constantly characterized [the bank's] conduct." If debtors did not respond satisfactorily, he ordered his officers to "put them into the hands of the Marshall accordingly."[8]

Perhaps his most severe reaction to an elusive debtor was aimed at Hugh Glenn, who owed the bank more than $117,000. Clay directed George Jones at the Cincinnati agency to get a writ from the court for arrest and imprisonment of Glenn. In fact, he wondered, how had Glenn already got a release from jail? Later, he heard that Glenn might come down the river in his boat. If he did, he instructed Jones to get a levy confiscating it.[9] That kind of remedy seemed to him justifiable, for he had been urging the legislature to authorize seizure of delinquent debtors' property.

A protracted, interesting case that Clay did not argue but closely monitored was *Piatt v Vattier.* It involved very valuable land and a hotel located in the center of Cincinnati. Sources indicate his continuing advice on how to handle the suit, which dragged on until a decision of the Supreme Court in favor of the BUS. The decision applied the statute of limitations to a fraudulent certificate of ownership that Robert Piatt had presented to the bank.[10]

The lawyer developed other strategies in collecting debts. One settlement was to receive a transfer of a company's assets in the form of debts owed to that company.[11] And he now considered even taking personal property to carry out judgments against debtors.[12]

Despite Clay's early reluctance for the bank to acquire real estate, he found it increasingly necessary, as large numbers of the bank's debtors had only that kind of collateral to comply with court executions. Too often, they were also delinquent in their tax payments and were forced to put their land up for sale. In some instances he instructed his agents to attend these tax auctions and to bid for the property. The situation bothered him as well as the owners. Besides the economic undesirability of the corporation's taking this course, it would generate even more hard feelings by the public. Nevertheless, his correspondence with the bank's agents, such as George Jones in Cincinnati, frequently gave them detailed instructions in handling land cases in court and in following up with more detailed directions on getting compliance. A flurry of letters to Jones concerned intricate litigation about certain land in Ohio, originally granted to John Cleves Symmes and now held by a relative. The attorney representing her, as well as Robert Piatt, was Nicholas Longworth. The bank tangled with Longworth, apparently not a very principled character, but Clay did prevail in this suit.[13]

He returned to Congress in December 1823, which reduced, though did not end, his professional work for the bank. He continued to advise Nicholas Biddle, now the corporation's president, about pending cases with which he was familiar. Indeed, he maintained the connection while he was a candidate during the complicated presidential election of 1824 and until he became secretary of state the following March.

In looking back upon the preceding four years, he felt proud of his record of success. In all but a very few of the hundreds of cases with which he had something to do, there was only a handful in which he or his associates failed to get a favorable court order, affirming the bank's legal right to collect. That is not to say that the eventual outcome of the cases was always complete compliance with the judgments, for there had to be compromises with distressed debtors; and there were, of course, innumerable evasions of payment.[14] Cheves, Biddle, and other bank executives generously praised his contributions and would often rely upon him in the future. He was also rewarded adequately in a monetary sense, at least to help him recoup his personal finances, though compared with the incomes of other prominent lawyers, his remuneration was modest.[15]

Still, did his role as a determined prosecutor of hapless debtors hurt him politically? Opinion in both Kentucky and Ohio was aroused against the bank, but not against Clay personally. One of his closest friends in Ohio was Charles Hammond, a prominent editor and legislator, who had strongly supported Clay's national policies and presidential hopes. However, he wrote a letter scolding the Kentuckian for using harsh tactics against debtors and for trampling the state's rights in the current *Osborn* case on taxing the bank. Clay must check these grievances, he warned. In referring to the coming election, he declared, "There are, I am persuaded, many who will feel it their duty to make opinions upon this subject something like a *sine qua non*."[16]

It is doubtful that there was much damage done to Clay the politician in 1824. In Kentucky he lost some votes for the presidency to Jackson, which probably reflected dissatisfaction with his disapproval of that state's relief laws but apparently not with his activity as lawyer in debt collection. Old Hickory's personal popularity must have been a more important factor. In Ohio a modern researcher studied original sources of information on Clay's bank cases and on voting in some counties, which did not indicate a significant correlation of law and politics unfavorable to him. In fact, he carried the state.[17]

During this period of his professional connection with the national bank, a fundamental question was the very existence of its offices throughout the country. A well-known instance of this issue was the case of *Osborn v Bank of the United States* (1824), coming up to the Supreme Court from Ohio; but the question had also arisen in several other states, especially in Maryland. As legal superintendent for the BUS in two states, Clay played an active role in handling the problem in Kentucky as well as Ohio. A downturn of the economy there tightened credit, created a banking crisis, depressed the condition of debtors, and induced angry attacks upon the two BUS branches at Lexington and Louisville as being largely responsible for hard times. Like other states, Kentucky laid a heavy annual tax, here of $60,000, on each branch with the obvious purpose of driving out the institution. Just as happened at the office in Maryland, the bank's reaction was refusal to pay this levy because of its unconstitutionality. When the *McCulloch* decision (1819) invalidated Maryland's taxation of the bank, the Kentucky courts retreated, and the trend of the controversy shifted against the institution's opponents.[18] While strongly disapproving his state's effort to tax the bank, Clay had believed time was on the side of the BUS and had predicted it would receive judicial support.[19]

His predictions were justified. One indication was a case he won in the Kentucky Court of Appeals, upholding the bank's authority to purchase and otherwise acquire promissory notes in the course of business with borrowers. This victory greatly strengthened its operation.[20]

Later in *Roberts v BUS* (1822) Clay had the opportunity to argue in the federal circuit court for the important right of the corporation's access as a party in suits before national tribunals. Winning here might be a large stride toward success in the similar jurisdictional case of *Osborn,* developing in Ohio and paving the way to the Supreme Court. The question in *Roberts* centered on a congressional law of 1816, chartering the national bank and conferring its standing in United States courts. Was this statute constitutional? Representing the BUS, Clay relied upon article 3, section 1, of the Constitution, extending the federal judicial power "to all Cases, in Law and Equity, arising under this Constitution, the Laws of the United States, and Treaties." Since the bank's charter was a law of the United States, Clay could convincingly contend it was decisive for his client. The judges agreed. They conceded there were hardly any precedents for their decision, but they remarked that they received "great assistance from arguments we have heard from the bar."[21]

Though generally this was a time when the numbers of defaulting debtors escalated, Clay cautiously avoided entanglement in Kentucky's highly explosive policy of relief for them. He clearly disapproved this legislation, postponing or otherwise moderating debtors' payments; but it was risky politically to counter the high tide of relief sentiment. He seldom took cases involving the measures. Not until the midtwenties did the anti-relief legislators and judges gain an upper hand. Meanwhile, he advised Biddle it was not in the bank's interest to challenge the constitutionality of these statutes. It would be better, he wrote, to give debtors more time and therefore stand a better chance of collection. He assured the BUS president he would supply information and suggestions to other counsel on handling such questions.[22] In the hundreds of cases for straight judicial execution of debtor liability which he did present, he proudly reported almost complete success in obtaining court orders.[23] Nevertheless, favorable rulings here, as in Ohio, did not always cause full or quick compliance.

By 1824 his activity as lawyer had centered on a crucial appeal to the Supreme Court involving Ohio's crippling taxation of BUS branches there. Over several years this intense constitutional dispute had developed out of economic conditions similar to those in Kentucky and several other states. Following the peace treaty of 1815, the state had experienced a boom. A surge of migration from South and East, mounting land-office sales, and ambitious projects of internal improvements led to a condition of financial overexpansion. The Ohio legislature had chartered many banks, twenty-three by 1818, generating a great flurry of loans while failing to require specie payment of their notes. Then two branch offices of the national bank set up business at Cincinnati and Chillicothe, trying to stabilize conditions but soon having to contract credit severely. The result was deep trouble for debtors whose mortgages were foreclosed. It was a particularly serious situation in the Cincinnati area where the BUS took over a very large amount of real estate. So one consequence of all this was attachment of blame for the crisis to that institution. It did not help to tell those who suffered that a panic and depression afflicted the country as a whole.[24]

The legislature responded to rising complaint in February 1819 with a statute laying a heavy annual tax of $50,000 on each of the two bank branches. If the bank refused to pay this tax, the law directed the state auditor to levy its funds and goods. It would probably leave Ohio, the sponsors of the legislation believed, rather than assume such a burden; and that would be a desirable outcome of the policy, since the exploitative corporation did not have the right to operate in their jurisdiction without permission. No matter what the national government did, this sovereign state had constitutional power to define its own authority on such questions, politicians insisted. But a few weeks later, the Supreme Court invalidated a similar tax in *McCulloch v Maryland* (1819), a heavy blow to other states resisting the BUS.[25]

Responsibility to collect the Ohio tax lay with the state auditor, Ralph Osborn, whose name would be permanently associated with this unusual legal episode. He confronted two contrary options. One was the bank's request for an injunction by the federal circuit court against collecting the tax. The other was a warrant by the state to collect the tax. He decided to ignore the possible injunction on the ground that the request for it was an incomplete petition, only to be served with a subpoena ordering his appearance in court. He would proceed to collect the tax.[26]

The auditor therefore directed Sheriff John Harper and an assistant to go at once to Chillicothe and seize $100,000 from the BUS branch. At this point in the weird story, as soon as the two men arrived, they jumped over the bank's counter, opened the vault, commandeered the money, loaded it in a wagon, and hurried back to Columbus, the capital. Here they turned their receipts over to the state treasurer, Samuel Sullivan. Again there was a hearing at the federal court on complaints of contempt and trespass, ending in jail time for both Harper and Sullivan. The bank also charged Osborn himself with contempt and trespass too.[27]

In strange proceedings John Wright, the United States district attorney, appeared not only as prosecutor for the federal government in this criminal case but also as one of the state defendants in it. Acting as the bank's attorney, Clay protested that the dual status was an obvious conflict of interest. He persuaded the court to name himself a prosecuting "solicitor" to assist

Wright, which gave him also dual status. Altogether, the situation was quite confusing. At any rate, the charge of contempt was dropped, leaving only trespass. By agreement of counsel, the money was turned over to commissioners, pending a decision by the Supreme Court's review of this dispute in Washington.[28]

At an earlier hearing, the circuit court had signaled what the outcome of that review might be. It rejected the state's argument that this was not merely a suit against Osborn as an individual but in effect against Ohio itself, which would be contrary to the Eleventh Amendment of the Constitution. Instead, the court adhered to the recent decision of the highest tribunal in *McCulloch,* invalidating Maryland's taxation of the national bank as a decisive precedent in the present case and disarming the resistant Osborn.[29]

Meanwhile, the legislature strengthened its attack. Charles Hammond's committee there issued a hard-line report, justifying the tax, however burdensome it may have been. Indeed, it was admittedly a penalty this private and unwelcome corporation must bear or preferably leave the state. To expedite the bank's departure, the committee recommended denying state protection of the bank's operations by refusing to record its property transactions officially and depriving it of remedies in Ohio courts. The panel would also withdraw the federal court's use of the state's jails. These penalties would amount to outlawry of the BUS.

Hammond then advanced a bold criticism of the Supreme Court's affirmation of the bank's constitutionality in the *McCulloch* case, when it invalidated state taxation. And he condemned the recent action of the federal circuit court in favor of the bank against Osborn and others. Ohio, he said, had greater power than these judges in interpreting the Constitution. His authority was the Virginia and Kentucky resolutions of 1798, the favorite scripture of states' rights Jeffersonians. The legislature voted overwhelming approval of the committee's recommendations, including one to circulate them among all the states as well as national officials and congressmen at Washington.[30]

This manifesto did not recruit much help across the country.

Even states that had been or would be advocates of a union based upon a loose compact of sovereign members did not come forward with concurrences. One of the few exceptions was Georgia, presently combatting the BUS branch in a controversy with its state bank in a federal circuit court. That tribunal's judges divided in opinion so that the case was certified to the Supreme Court and would be decided with *Osborn*.[31]

At least one state, Massachusetts, expressed strong disapproval of Hammond's states' rights exegesis. Apparently shaped by Daniel Webster, adopted by his legislature, and noticed nationally, the rebuttal criticized Ohio for deviation from correct constitutional theory. The congressional charter of the national bank, a United States statute, was the supreme law of the land, state policy to the contrary notwithstanding. And Ohio's reliance upon the Eleventh Amendment as immunity from the corporation's suit did not protect its officials who employed an unconstitutional measure. More would be heard from Webster when he became one of the bank's attorneys in the appeal of *Osborn* to the Supreme Court.[32]

An interesting reaction to these events came from Hezekiah Niles's *Weekly Register,* which was publishing a great deal of information about them for its many readers at the time and for later historians. A longstanding critic of the national bank, Niles agreed with much of Ohio's complaints against a heartless BUS treatment of state banks and of debtors. He believed Congress should authorize state taxation in order to clarify the boundaries of power. Nevertheless, the editor decidedly disapproved rash state action because the situation was one of legal controversy and not of forcible remedy. As a serious question of constitutional law, he said, the dispute demanded peaceful and constructive consideration. It was good advice, but it did not pacify many Ohioans.[33]

The detention of state officers who had seized the bank's funds raised questions for Clay. Harper and others had been held in a local jail for some months and later filed a bill in a state court for false imprisonment. Clay knew that this would be a friendly forum for these officers and therefore considered how to transfer their case to a federal tribunal, preferably the Supreme Court. This could be done by the process of removal to it at the outset or by an appeal there after a state decision. As it happened, neither effort was necessary as the issue became moot.[34] He would not have had to worry about the state system of justice if there had been a federal prison in Ohio to which the federal circuit court could have assigned violators of its rulings. This difficulty had increased as a result of legislative outlawry of the bank, denying the use of state jails for prisoners committed under United States authority. But his concerns lessened when he got a measure through Congress that provided funds for hiring "a convenient place to serve as a temporary jail."[35]

Another bothersome effect of outlawry would stop official recording and validating the bank's operations. Clay instructed BUS solicitors how to respond to this obstruction. If they submitted documents to be recorded by state officers or judges who refused, he said, the attorneys should obtain a written statement from them. The refusal itself could be used then or later with federal help for proof of authenticity. He did believe that judicial relief from this vexation was near.[36]

There were also signs of some kind of settlement of the controversy by the two sides. In negotiations with Clay during January 1821, Hammond reported action by the legislature and proposals for a compromise. The state would reduce the combined annual tax on the two branches from $100,000, which had been seized, to $5,000 and would return the difference to the bank. But Clay understood that the principle of a tax would remain and that the only way to avoid it would be to leave Ohio. So he rejected this sort of offer.[37] A month later, the lower house of the legislature did pass a bill to restore the BUS funds without conditions, but the upper chamber amended it to require withdrawal of the branch offices. "As we have exhausted the cup of conciliation," Clay declared, "nothing remains to us but to proceed firmly & temperately in our purpose. That shall be done, and in September next, if I live, we will have a Judgment or decree, or both for the money." [38]

Cheves and his successor as bank president, Nicholas Biddle, praised Clay's management of the case, assured him the board of directors was entirely satisfied, provided him with a liberal compensation for his representation in the Ohio courts, and promised more for the pending appeal to the Supreme Court.

Despite delay through 1823, he was pleased with the shape of questions the high court would decide, particularly that of state taxation of the branches, contrary to the *McCulloch* rule. Of course, the more difficult issue, he thought, was whether the federal circuit court had correctly assumed jurisdiction over an injunction to Osborn, a state official, perhaps amounting to an unconstitutional suit against the state itself.[39]

At last, in February 1824, he argued the case for the bank in the Supreme Court. Charles Hammond and John Wright, the prominent Ohioans involved in this controversy from the beginning, were formidable opponents and made a powerful plea for the state's policy. Clay alone appeared for the bank, but a few days later, Chief Justice Marshall requested further argument on the issue of the circuit court's jurisdiction. He also ordered that the similar case from Georgia be considered along with *Osborn*. Then other lawyers joined Wright on the appeal, while Daniel Webster and John Sergeant, both stalwart BUS attorneys, appeared with Clay in the second hearing.

Counsel for Osborn emphasized the Eleventh Amendment's prohibition of federal suits commenced against a state (Ohio) by citizens of another state (the bank corporation). They connected this provision to the ancient doctrine of sovereign immunity of a government from litigation without its consent. Though an injunction had been only nominally issued against Osborn and other individuals, they contended it was, in effect, an unconstitutional suit against the state. They also cited precedents consistently denying corporations, such as the bank, the standing of citizenship as parties in federal courts.

Clay's opponents added a rather hopeless call for reversal of Marshall's holding in *McCulloch*, depriving states of the power to tax the institution.[40] Clay felt quite comfortable about the durability of that ruling, as well he might in John Marshall's court. This was true of his argument at the first hearing when he appeared alone for the bank and more so in the combined argument with Webster and Sergeant at the second hearing. On both occasions, he focused on the question of whether the federal circuit court had jurisdiction. Its injunction was properly directed to Osborn individually, not to the state of Ohio, he insisted. Even though the state was affected by the order to return the seized funds to the bank, Ohio was not formally a party of record in the case. Osborn himself had been therefore identified correctly as the defendant. The chief justice must have been listening carefully when Clay advanced this point.[41]

The lawyer also emphasized the precedent of *U.S. v Peters* (1809), a Supreme Court decision. In an old controversy over possession of proceeds from a prize ship, the federal circuit judge in Pennsylvania, Richard Peters, had met resistance by aroused officials who opposed his ordering a return of the assets to certain claimants rather than to the state. The cautious Peters refrained from finally executing his decision for these claimants, and an appeal to get him to do it went to the Supreme Court. It became clear that the state was the key element in the dispute and might invoke the Eleventh Amendment to prevent commencement of a suit in federal court against it by out-of-state claimants. To sidestep the amendment's barrier, Marshall's opinion made Judge Peters instead of the state the defendant and ordered him to make the award to the claimants. So Peters was the formal party of record but not the real target. The outcome was to bypass Pennsylvania, unlikely to acquiesce in an adverse award. Here was a possible parallel with *Osborn*, which could restrict Ohio, even though Ralph Osborn individually was the party of record. It was a useful strategy to shape the record of a case according to circumstances.[42]

Clay brought in *Cohens v Virginia* (1821) as another precedent to define the Eleventh Amendment. But he made little progress with it since it was not an original suit "commenced" against a state, as the language of the amendment specified. Instead, it was an appeal to the high court after prosecution of persons by a state, which had commenced a controversy. Still, *Cohens* did lay out the broad dimensions of a law of the United States superior to a law of a state in Marshall's best version of constitutional nationalism. Clay saw this much in *Cohens* applicable to *Osborn*. He directed attention to the congressional charter of the bank in 1816, a law of the United States. It granted the corporation the valuable right to sue or defend cases in the federal circuit courts. This provision, he said, was a valid derivative from the Constitution, article 3, section 2, extending the national judicial power to "all Cases, in Law and Equity, arising under the Constitution, and the Laws of the United States." And article 6 made national statutes "the supreme Law of the Land . . . anything in the Constitution or Laws of any State to the Contrary notwithstanding." As in *Cohens,* the Supreme Court's jurisdiction in *Osborn* must prevail over that of a state.[43]

It was odd that Clay did not specifically urge the court to follow the precedent of the *Roberts* case, which he had won for the bank in the federal circuit court in Kentucky. He was, of course, very much aware of its relevance in assuring the bank access to national courts, and it is probable the chief justice was too.[44]

Now Marshall delivered a long opinion soon after argument had ended. It was a typically bold exposition of the Constitution but included some dubious comments on how the court should handle suits attacking state laws. Nevertheless, his disposition of the case pleased Clay entirely.

On the question of jurisdiction of federal courts in suits against a state by a party from another state, he reduced the potential coverage accorded it by the Eleventh Amendment. Though conceding protection for the state if directly named as a party in the action's title, the chief justice did not offer much if the suit were brought against a state official, such as Osborn. The state would have to be the party of record in the case, technically appearing as defendant, not merely having an important interest in the outcome. But Osborn, not Ohio, had been identified as the defendant on the record, and therefore he could not claim immunity. Exactly what Clay and his colleagues had contended. That formula was too mechanical and probably unfair, squeezing the official between duty to the state and compulsion by federal judges.

Marshall had surer footing when he drew upon the bank's charter, a law of the United States, which conferred to it the privilege of suit and defense in the nation's circuit courts. He gave the charter the broadest interpretation, indeed for all operations as a financial corporation. His authority was article 3 of the Constitution, establishing the national judicial power over all questions arising under that document and the laws of the United States.

The most significant but least surprising holding in Marshall's opinion adhered to the *McCulloch* precedent. Like Maryland, Ohio could not tax the national bank because it was the fiscal agent of the federal government, he declared again. It held deposits and made disbursements of the Treasury, assisted in issuance and retirement of bonds, circulated its notes serving as the country's prevalent currency, and coordinated operations of state banks, "all necessary and proper" constitutional functions, related to delegated congressional powers, not to be hindered by taxation.[45]

Justice William Johnson dissented, as he occasionally did. Though expressing approval of the bank and disapproval of state interference, he worried about potential limits on jurisdiction of state courts. He wondered why such cases as *Osborn* should not first go to those tribunals, always later subject to review by the Supreme Court. Though complicating the judicial process, that alternative might have yielded some useful insights into local circumstances.[46]

The effects of the *Osborn* decision were mixed. Marshall's rigid emphasis upon the formal party of record did not always have clear-cut applications. Shortly afterward he disposed of another case rather differently. In this suit against a state governor, who was the party of record, he rejected jurisdiction because the action was really aimed at the state, not that official personally—seemingly a reversal of direction.[47] And through the years, the Court found exceptions to a simple formula of sovereign immunity based on the Eleventh Amendment. It might find the party of record a nominal instead of the actual target and was willing to look into factual considerations.[48] In an era of extensive state economic regulation, it invoked the expanding contract and due process clauses of the Constitution to restrict enforcement of legislation despite the Eleventh Amendment. And it held repeatedly that a state could not claim sovereign immunity if relying upon an unconstitutional law. The court later responded to questions in some ways that Marshall the conservative judge and Clay the conservative lawyer could have found productive.[49]

Besides the Bank of the United States, Clay had a long relationship with state banks in Kentucky, beginning soon after his arrival in the West. As stockholder, board member, and lawyer, he prominently served and influenced several of these institutions. In the twenties and thirties he was especially involved in the operations of the Bank of the Commonwealth of Kentucky. A highlight was his representation as its counsel in the well-known case of *Briscoe v Bank of Kentucky* (1837).

To understand his connection with this decision, one must look back to 1820 when he attended a meeting of that bank's directors. He successfully presented a resolution to obtain renewal of the institution's state charter, but his other resolutions, calling for more conservative policies on reserves, note issues, and loans, all to protect the public against suspension of specie payment, failed adoption.[50] Trouble lay ahead as a depression intensified, putting the bank in an increasingly weak position. With little capital it issued ever more paper with dwindling reserves to redeem it.

This situation and Clay's feelings were well illustrated by his own financial difficulty, partly due to his acquisition of large amounts of Bank of Kentucky notes in the early twenties. Failing to get these notes redeemed in specie, he agreed to accept from the bank the personal notes it had received from debtors. But he could not get these notes redeemed either.[51] He then tried to exchange the bank paper at the Lexington branch of the BUS, but Biddle informed him the board of directors at Philadelphia rejected his request.[52] He later expressed his dissatisfaction in plain language: "Our paper bank in Kentucky has so far disappointed the hopes of the public that everybody is tired of it and desirous to get back, as soon as we can, to a specie circulation."[53] Clay surely remembered the bank's sorry record for a long while, especially in 1837 when, as its counsel in the Supreme Court, he argued *Briscoe v Bank of Kentucky.*

The case arose from this very practice of circulating irredeemable bank notes. It involved a loan made by the bank in these notes and later nonpayment by the debtor, John Briscoe, who challenged their validity. His counsel contended they were mere paper, amounting to bills of credit, supported only by the state's credit and good faith. He reasoned that the bank was the creature and agent of the state. Its corporate charter authorized the state to select its officers, subscribe all its stock, and generally control its operations. So the state's resort to this kind of notes was unconstitutional, because it was prohibited from issuing bills of credit by a clause in article 1, section 10.[54]

In preparing argument for the bank in *Briscoe,* Clay had to devise a way to counter a recent decision of the Marshall court in *Craig v Missouri* (1830), holding that loan certificates issued by that state were bills of credit and therefore constitutionally prohibited. Intended as a medium of payment for taxes and debts to the state and for salaries to state employees but not for legal tender in all circumstances, some certificates had nevertheless found their way into general circulation. In a characteristically nationalist, conservative opinion, the chief justice had ruled the Missouri certificates to be bills of credit. He had reviewed financial history as far back as the era of the Revolution to demonstrate troublesome effects of such policies. The value of that kind of medium had constantly fluctuated, he declared, and had caused immense losses, ruinous speculations, and destruction of "all confidence between man and man."

In the minority of the four-to-three decision, William Johnson had thought the certificates were not a circulating medium; furthermore, he had found no precise meaning of the term "bills of credit." Smith Thompson had also dissented with a worrisome reference to bank notes in all the states as a large component of the currency of the country. Would the court also declare them invalid? McLean, dissenting too, had wondered about that possibility. Nevertheless, while hearing cases in the federal circuit court of Kentucky, he had not caused the bank any trouble about its notes.[55]

For the *Briscoe* hearing, Clay could count on an encouraging realignment of the court. Though one of the dissenters in *Craig,* Johnson, was no longer on the bench, the other two, Thompson and McLean, were. Marshall had died and was replaced as chief justice by the arch Jacksonian states' righter Roger Taney. And two more Democratic appointees, Philip Barbour and James Wayne, made up a majority of at least five justices among the seven who would sit in the forthcoming case in 1837 and might bypass *Craig.* What a peculiar situation for the staunch nationalist Clay to advance state power over banks and attract such assistance from members of the political party with which he had long done battle about banking! Would Story, learned veteran from the Marshall court, be the only dissenter since the tables were turned?

Other help for Clay to win the bank's cause had been the outcome of a hearing on it before the high tribunal in 1834, three years earlier. The proceedings were merely mentioned in the court report but predictive of a new direction. Only five of the seven members sat, and the vote of three to two against the Bank of Kentucky was one vote short of the required majority of the full court of seven. After this fortunate escape by Clay's side, the case was carried over to the term of 1837 for the more friendly Taney court to decide.[56]

For appellant Briscoe, Joseph White and Samuel Southard urged the court to apply *Craig* as precedent. Like Missouri's loan office, they contended, the bank as Kentucky's agent was circulating unconstitutional bills of credit as legal tender. Southard, a close political friend of Clay, knew the vulnerable spots in his record. During hard times the Kentuckian had opposed the state's ill-advised chartering of numerous wildcat banks, such as the so-called forty thieves. And he had strongly criticized loose practices of the Bank of Kentucky in floating irredeemable paper and lacking sufficient reserves, said Southard. It was all a part of the relief program he had opposed in those days. But now he was an advocate for the same financial institution.[57]

In his argument Clay emphasized a separation of the bank from the state. It was a corporation issuing its own notes, not those of the state, he said, so that the constitutional prohibition of state bills of credit would be inapplicable. The Kentucky institution's paper resembled that of all state-created banks in the country. If the court took the opposite view, Clay predicted, the notes of these banks would be endangered, a frightening possibility because of the widespread use of this medium in the economy. Still, his questionable depiction of the Kentucky corporation's functions as independent of its creator was crucial to his case.[58] Yet he seemed to reach rather far by referring to an earlier decision in which the Supreme Court did find a close relationship of the two but refrained from ruling against it.[59] He finished with a call for judicial restraint: "Keep to the plain meaning of the terms of the constitution, and do not seek, by construction, to include in its prohibitions, such paper as that which is brought into question in this case, and all will be safe."[60]

Justice McLean delivered the court's opinion. One of the dissenters in *Craig*, he now spoke for a decided majority. His views were well settled, no doubt all the more because he had attended the federal circuit court in Kentucky where this subject had been prominent. He did concede there was an intimate connection of bank and state, beyond what Clay had allowed. The corporation's charter, he said, allowed the state to select bank officers, to hold all its stock, and to issue notes, which were declared by law to be acceptable in various kinds of payments. Nevertheless, he ruled they were not bills of credit and offered a rather weak explanation that the notes were merely necessary measures for economic relief. They were not intended to supply legal tender, he added inconsistently. Like Clay, McLean seemed to be quite worried about a decision against Kentucky's notes spreading to bank notes in other states.[61]

Story, the only dissenter, displayed his well-known ability in an animated opinion. He remarked that Marshall had twice heard argument on the present question and in both instances had a majority with him, once when invalidating state notes in *Craig* and later in the first *Briscoe* hearing though lacking a quorum on the bench. Regretting that the chief justice could not now speak for himself, Story felt obliged to "vindicate his memory." Specifically, he disagreed with Clay's contention that the bank and the state were distinctly separate, so that the corporation's notes were not state bills of credit. Instead, Story declared, the state had its agent, the bank, issue them, and they circulated as money. Look at the initial pleas in the case, he urged, and you will find the bank admitted it had issued bills of credit and promised to pay them in behalf of the state. In general, Story declared he would not uphold a practice to do something indirectly by assigning a false name to it when it was a direct circumvention of constitutional law.[62]

In winning this case, Clay had indeed resorted to some weak logic. His contention that the Commonwealth Bank of Kentucky was a corporation separate from the state was inaccurate. The bank was far from independent of the state. Just the opposite. Notes were nominally issued by the corporation, but Story was correct in complaining that the effect was to issue state bills of credit. And the state could do so because it owned all the bank's stock, chose its officers, and controlled its operations.[63] The majority decision extended into the 1830s an accommodation the state had provided to its hard pressed bank during the twenties. But as Clay and others said during the court's hearing of *Briscoe*, the bank had now recovered and was redeeming its notes on a sound basis. An important long-range effect of the decision was to reduce the likelihood that state-bank paper would be invalidated as an established medium of exchange in the country's economy. Judges and lawyers emphasized this point. Yet they could not know that within weeks, in early 1837, a severe financial panic would afflict the land and introduce a long-range depression. State bank notes lost quality whatever the court had said. And three decades later, they would be driven from circulation altogether by national policy.[64]

In assessing two of Clay's constitutional cases in the Supreme Court, *Osborn* and *Briscoe*, in behalf of national and state banks, one sees a lawyer well-informed about financial and legal subjects, reflecting his own involvement in their political dimensions. His perspective was that of a conservative who valued economic growth, understandable in light of his personal experience in Kentucky from an early date and of his long activity in the national arena where issues had constitutional importance.

During the 1820s Clay had been quite busy as counsel for the BUS in charge of collecting debts in western states. During an economic recession there was much to do to handle resulting legal and political problems. This at a time on the national scene when the Jacksonian attack upon the institution as a monster would soon prevail on the question of renewing its charter. Clay led the bank's weakening defense in Congress on that issue.

His early approach to collecting debts to the bank was rather lenient, no doubt influenced by general economic conditions. It was not only a realistic response to them but also an effort to check long-range hostility of the public. In Kentucky particularly, he faced the anti-bank discontent that had led to the controversial policy of debtor relief. Though disliking those measures, he was circumspect in advancing his negative opinion.

His strategy gradually tightened. He developed a system involving action in the courts, both state and federal. He kept in close touch with the bank's agents at the branches in Ohio. By his instructions, they filed suits to foreclose mortgages transferring assets, much of it land, to the BUS. Judicial orders were issued against debtors in large numbers, notwithstanding evasions and obstructions. No wonder the corporation had been widely labeled the monster. Clay himself carried out this move in the Kentucky courts while instructing his agents in Ohio. It was there that popular resistance led into the key case of *Osborn.*

Now he took over the litigation involving the state's auditor, who had enforced the law of Ohio for seizure of bank funds from crippling taxes. Clay's work in the federal circuit court was well handled. He got an injunction forbidding this taxation and a ruling for jurisdiction concerning unconstitutional actions of Osborn personally, not the state. In the long run, that was the most significant issue, depending on a ground-breaking interpretation of the Eleventh Amendment. Gaining a decision here that the suit was against an individual not the state itself, prohibited by that amendment, he moved on to the Supreme Court, a promising setting for affirming this answer to the question.

Even more promising was the prospect of Chief Justice Marshall's adhering to his recent conclusion in the *McCulloch* case that a state could not tax and therefore destroy the national bank as an arm of the government. And he did reiterate it. So Clay's principal concern remained the meaning of the Eleventh Amendment. Was the present case a prohibited suit against a state or was it what its title indicated: a suit against Ralph Osborn, responsible for an unconstitutional act? In insisting that the case was against Osborn, Clay and his colleagues offered, to some extent, an artificial, pro forma definition instead of a careful factual analysis of the real character of the so-called "party of record." An alternative path Clay could have followed would have been to rely upon *Roberts v BUS* (1822), his recent federal circuit case in Kentucky, recognizing the standing of the national bank as a party in that tribunal. *Roberts* upheld the Bank's right on the basis of its congressional charter, a law of the United States, carrying with it access to and protection of the national courts. Article 3 of the Constitution confers jurisdiction in such cases. That was the core of his argument now. But it is unclear why he and the chief justice did not cite *Roberts* because both of them could recall it well. Perhaps he thought it unnecessary to develop his present argument.

Another instance of the close relationship of banking and constitutional law was *Briscoe,* an obvious circumvention of the clause prohibiting state bills of credit. In representing the Bank of Kentucky, Clay seemed out of character. Unconvincingly he denied it was a state agency in ownership and operation when it issued its notes, quite obviously the kind of currency forbidden. And Clay knew it. This at a time when the Jacksonian political faith promoted the option of state banks instead of a national bank, favored by Clay and his party. His opponent during the hearing, Samuel Southard, who knew him well, exploited his inconsistencies, but not enough to deter the justices from deciding for the state bank. The determining point in the outcome, as Clay and several members of the court emphasized, was the practical need to retain the general circulation of state paper. That would hold true for a long while.

Though Clay had entered the political arena as a young man at the beginning of the nineteenth century with strong reservations about the Federalist-sponsored First Bank of the United States, even voting against renewal of its charter, he later became a very important recruit among its supporters. His role also as a regular attorney for the bank after 1815 was a substantial asset for the corporation, and as a party leader he included the BUS as a pillar in his economic policy, known as the American System. During the early twenties as a lawyer, he contributed a great deal to the rising strength of the institution. In state and national courts he helped establish its valuable legal status.

5

NONCONSTITUTIONAL BUSINESS

Some of Clay's legal practice involved constitutional questions, such as the boundaries of state power over banking and contracts, often in relation to national power. Notwithstanding the great significance of these subjects, Clay and fellow lawyers participated in many more nonconstitutional cases. The Supreme Court in John Marshall's day (1801–35), for example, decided twelve times as many nonconstitutional as constitutional questions.[1]

A frequent subject in that litigation was land. It arose from disputes about titles administered by states and conveyances accomplished by sale or will, all in a bewildering, disorderly setting of public policy. Clay's cases had these characteristics. His preparation and personal interest emphasized the relationship of the law and land. It was here that his experience and skill advanced his reputation at the bar. And more than his political service or his own agricultural interest, this branch of legal business enhanced his income. In fact, much of it in the early years consisted of large parcels of land instead of monetary fees from his clients.

Predictably, land law in early nineteenth-century America was a mixture of the old and the new. What little the lawyers and judges learned from professional instruction often drew upon

English commentaries and reports, whose rules on tenancy, titles, deeds, mortgages, and estates moved slowly away from feudal to modern structures. An influence upon these pragmatic applications was a great variety of state land policies or lack of them. In Kentucky and elsewhere the confusion of acquisition and use of land generated complicated legal questions, as Clay's case of *Green v Biddle* (1823) in the Supreme Court had illustrated. It was not an isolated instance of these tangled systems, if one dare use the term "system." Then an important national dimension was also developing from congressional legislation on public lands, which brought more problems.[2]

One of Clay's early land cases, *McConnell v Brown* (1821), shows the complicated character of this part of his practice. In 1786 Edmund Taylor had received for his military service a Virginia grant of five thousand acres in Kentucky before its separation from the Old Dominion. His will provided that this land go to his children in equal shares, and at Taylor's death his son supposedly distributed it that way. Actually, other persons filed suit, contending that the younger Taylor had also sold some tracts to them. They prevailed in a county court against Clay's client, who had relied upon the will, contrary to such transactions. But the Kentucky appellate court reversed the decision. In rejecting Clay's argument resting upon the validity of the will, the state chief justice handed down an opinion that the entire bequest was void. When the will for equal distribution of land among Taylor's children was drawn up, he ruled, Virginia law required primogeniture, all such inherited property to go to the eldest son. He had violated that requirement by sale of some of the land. So Clay lost his case, and both parties lost some land.[3]

Like many reports of this appellate court, there is no citation to precedents or other authorities in the opinion. In fact, there is little information on the substance of Clay's argument. But the most interesting aspect of the outcome is the free judicial application of the feudal rule of primogeniture in an American republic.

Another example of lingering premodern doctrine is *Kirk v Smith* (1824)—and this in Marshall's Supreme Court. It involved extensive territory granted by the English crown in the seventeenth century to William Penn, the original proprietor of lands that his grandson John Penn now claimed as manors, still subject to the proprietary institution of quitrents. Killian Smith occupied such a manor in York County, Pennsylvania after a successful suit against another claimant, Caleb Kirk, in a federal circuit court. Kirk had lost in his reliance upon state laws which confiscated extensive tracts held by loyalists during the Revolution. Now he appealed to the Supreme Court and retained Clay and Daniel Webster as his counsel to overturn that decision favoring Smith and the proprietary interest.

Clay and Webster were well prepared. They made a full exposition of the relevant state legislation, especially a statute of 1779. Though they contended it rightly confiscated the proprietary interest and supported Kirk's claim, they suggested a modest compromise to allow part of it to Penn and Smith. A fine distinction could at least assure the occupancy and use of the land to Kirk at issue in this case. It would only permit the proprietor to attempt to collect some quitrents from manors. That was hardly promising to Smith and Penn, and their counsel so declared in a negative reply.[4]

Marshall handed down the majority opinion, long-winded and supportive of vested rights. After reviewing all relevant Pennsylvania statutes, especially the land-confiscation act of 1779, he held they did not interfere with Smith's continued occupancy of his manor, as granted by the Penns, who retained quitrent rights. The chief justice found no constitutional issue in the controversy and did not seriously examine the jurisdictional basis for hearing the appeal, seemingly only the need for the high court to review and affirm a decision for Smith by a lower federal tribunal. Only Justice William Johnson dissented, yet so unclearly that his opinion could have gone to either party.[5]

Overall, the importance of the case is to illustrate the Supreme Court's conservatism, adhering to old concepts in the important area of land law. In this instance, Marshall's approval of Smith's existing possession of a proprietary manor, as decided by the circuit court, reflected judicial restraint favoring his vested rights—not those of Clay's party, Kirk.

At the next term of the Court the lawyer fared better in *Elmendorf v Taylor* (1825) concerning the validity of title to a large tract of eight thousand acres in Kentucky, quaintly described as located between Floyd's Fork and Bull Skin. Typical of that period, this was a very uncertain boundary, though the record of the case described it as having been surveyed many years earlier. But an even greater problem was the admitted fact that Lucas Elmendorf had never entered title at the land office. For that reason he lost his claim in the federal circuit court. It was then that Clay agreed to represent him in an appeal to the Supreme Court. Argument by counsel and the chief justice's opinion were lengthy, citing numerous authorities and precedents, more of this by Marshall than one would have expected in view of his preference for broad generalizations and principles.

The opinion closely followed Clay's reasoning that the validity of a title could depend only upon a survey, which announced possession, fulfilled the essential legal requirement of notoriety of ownership, and therefore justified the "presumption" it had been recorded. It was quite a lenient decision.[6]

Some years later, Clay brought an unusual land case, *Livingston v Story* (1835–37), up to the post-Marshall Court. It arose in New Orleans and involved Edward Livingston, well-known Jacksonian Democrat and distinguished compiler of the civil law, which Louisiana had largely adopted instead of the common law found in the rest of the country. One of a prominent New York family, Livingston not only had an important political career in national office as senator, secretary of state, and minister to France but also had been quite active in the economic development of New Orleans, including the strip along the river-front levee, known as the batture. Pressed for capital in 1822, he borrowed $23,000 from Benjamin Story on the security of that property but did not repay the loan when it was due a year later. So Story kept possession of the mortgaged land, increasingly valuable due to an extensive program of constructing commercial buildings there. Despite not retiring the loan after a dozen years, Livingston protested that Story had improperly collected over $60,000 in rents and other profits from the tract.

Finally, he decided to file a bill of complaint in the federal district court in the city for a decree ordering Story to return his land and present an account of his profits. Livingston's motion asked that the judge employ the procedure of equity, a branch of the common law, in granting his request. The federal district judge ruled that his court did not have jurisdiction for invoking equity because his court had to employ procedures of the state's civil code, not of the common law. So Livingston appealed that decision to the Supreme Court. Then Story asked Clay to argue his defense at the 1835 term. A frequent visitor in New Orleans, with friends and relatives there, the lawyer was pleased to be retained in the case. Besides, he had no sympathy for Livingston, that minion of President Andrew Jackson, his perennial political foe.[7]

At this hearing, Clay urged affirming the lower court's decree, which denied jurisdiction. He emphasized an incompatibility of the equity procedures requested by Livingston and the well-settled civil code prevailing in Louisiana. These two incongruous legal systems could not operate together, and if compelled to choose between them, the people of Louisiana would firmly reject the common law, he declared.

Livingston's counsel concentrated on this jurisdictional question. The federal court's ruling was wrong, they argued, because it did have authority to employ the procedure of equity, granted by several congressional laws from the admission of the state in 1812 to the present. On that ground the decision of the Supreme Court went to Livingston, who could recover his land and money from Story, Clay's client. This majority opinion in 1835 came from Justice Smith Thompson, who had been Livingston's political friend during their earlier days in New York.[8]

At the term two years later in 1837, the lawyers reargued this question of jurisdictional boundaries, but with the same settlement of the controversy. The majority opinion now came from Justice James Wayne, another Jacksonian Democrat friendly to

Livingston. On the other hand, Justice Henry Baldwin, Clay's close friend, wrote a vigorous dissent, objecting to prejudicial treatment of Story's rights and to substituting common-law rules for the civil code in reluctant Louisiana. Political persuasions could filter into the law. As for the financial impact, the decision ordered the district court to refer questions to an appointed master in equity to make allowances for Livingston's previous payments on the principal to Story, but also for Story's obligation now to pay Livingston interest of eighteen percent for possession of the property from 1823 to the present, 1837. Livingston himself did not have the satisfaction of collecting that huge amount. He had died the previous year.

As for the legal issues, congressional legislation on the state's court system seems to have been sufficient to approve the district court's use of common law and equity, contrary to Clay's determined arguments. The Constitution authorizes Congress to establish courts with broad judicial power over cases in law and equity, arising under United States laws (article 3, sections 1 and 2). And Congress had passed laws from 1812 onward concerning the courts within Louisiana. These measures were credibly interpreted as assigning jurisdiction in cases of equity to them. Furthermore, though federal circuit courts in much of the country had heard cases involving national law, federal district courts in some states lacking a circuit judge increasingly did too. And the Supreme Court now ruled in the *Livingston* case that the district court in Louisiana could handle such cases in the absence of a circuit court. It could therefore grant relief to Livingston.[9]

An ironic feature of this controversy had been Livingston's resort to the common-law procedure of equity instead of the civil code of the state, which represented much of his own expert contribution. It would be interesting to know how he might have explained this apparent inconsistency.

At this term, when he argued *Livingston*, Clay appeared in another waterfront case. It was *New Orleans v De Armas and Cucullu,* in which Clay's clients claimed land based upon an old Spanish patent, upheld by the federal district court and a United

States law. On the other side, the city also claimed it as the site of a public wharf, protected by a superior authority of the treaty of the Louisiana Purchase (1803). When Clay took the case to the Supreme Court, he was able to build upon the chief justice's known caution about judicial interference in diplomatic affairs, due to constitutional separation of powers. Marshall predictably delivered an opinion that his court did not have jurisdiction in a law suit to intervene in these kinds of legislative and executive spheres. This meant he would not use the treaty to override the claims of Armas and Cucullu, and Clay won his case.[10]

Additional legal business in Louisiana concerned his relatives, James Brown and spouse, Ann Hart Brown, sister of Clay's wife Lucretia. A well-to-do politician and lawyer, Brown had acquired a good deal of land, including a plantation along the Mississippi and much property in town. When he and Ann died in the early 1830s, Clay helped manage and professionally defend their estates. He was executor of Ann's will, which had especially complicated problems.

A determined challenge to Brown's holdings had begun even before his death. Richard Keene filed suit against him in the federal district court in New Orleans. At issue was a contract between the two, which could transfer to him ownership of a valuable plot along the levee. Clay argued a defense for Brown against Keene, who failed to prove his diversity of citizenship and the right to sue in an appeal to the Supreme Court. He persisted in litigation for seven more years, then lost in another case. Clay saved $35,000 for the Brown estate.[11]

Seventeen years passed before removal of the last barrier to a final settlement of Ann Brown's estate, for which Clay was counsel and still executor. She had bequeathed a sizeable sum to her nephew John Humphreys, who, sad to say, did not live long enough to collect it.[12] It was, at last, possible to round out the remainder of Ann's estate. Lucretia got something, and Clay did too from his lawyer's fees. He shared that with his son Henry Junior, now a fresh attorney in the closing phase of hearings.

Particularly in land cases turning on the administration of

wills, Clay displayed a sound if not exhaustive command of the relevant law. One that attracted popular attention was *Singleton v Singleton* (1847). His suit in behalf of two children, aged eight and eleven, challenged the will of their grandfather Jeconias, who had devised his lands to the children's father, Elijah, as tenant for life. The court of Woodford County, Kentucky, had decreed that the will remained valid because children of such tender age could not be parties in the case. Clay devoted an unusual amount of time in presenting the suit before the state appellate court, which reversed the lower court's decree by approving standing of the children to challenge the will. It examined relevant state and English laws in detail, more so than customary. One can believe that the opinion borrowed liberally from Clay's extensive argument, though it was not reported.[13]

A selection of Clay's less prominent land cases shows characteristics of his practice and relates to the legal history of his time. He argued many of them in his state's high court but a number in federal circuit and supreme courts.

One type of these suits in which Clay was counsel arose from problems about early titles and boundaries of grants by Virginia in the part of the West which later became the present states of Ohio and Kentucky. Some of them concerned old land warrants, awarded to veterans of military service during the Revolution. The area lay north of the Ohio River between its branches, the Little Miami and the Scioto. But exact locations were unclear and often disputed, even after federal surveys, reports, and legislation. Receiving a large fee of four hundred acres out of a claim of seven hundred, Clay successfully carried *Doddridge v Thompson* (1824) to the Supreme Court. Marshall's long opinion, including a history of the military tracts, came to conclusions favorable to the claims of veterans. He was, of course, a Revolutionary veteran himself. At any rate, he held that, though lacking concrete proof, the general rule in these questions must be to assume that claims had been made in timely fashion prior to congressional legislation on the subject, as required. It could have been a dubious assumption.[14]

Marshall's perspective brought another loose-constructionist decision on military warrants, which Clay had successfully argued in the federal circuit of Ohio, though not appearing in the appeal to the Supreme Court. *Taylor v Myers* (1822) upheld the right of a person who was not the original holder of a land warrant to acquire land abandoned by a military grantee, and to do so even after passage of a law that would make the purchase too late. The right of abandonment, he held, must prevail over the statutory restriction. This interpretation opened more opportunities for transactions of speculators, such as Clay's party in the case.[15]

In several land cases Clay did not win or lose completely. It was characteristic of the judicial process in those days to use courts as mediators to accommodate rights and interests of opposing parties, especially concerning contracts and debts. As the lawyer once remarked in arguing a complex case, it was "a contest of two equities." Litigation moved slowly over as much as ten or twenty years, sometimes where tangled and puzzling evidence hindered a fair result. Such seemed true in *Watts v Waddle* (1832), involving town lots in Chillicothe. Clay's client, Watts, got a judgment in the Supreme Court, but Waddle got credit for rents and profits. That had been the kind of outcome Clay would soon see in *Livingston*. Decisions could amount to a "compromise."[16] It was so expressed in the state appellate court reporter's headnote for *Bates v Todd's Heirs* (1823), a difficult case, depending upon a promised transfer of 6,000 acres in Fayette County. Only a portion of the disputed tract went to each party.[17] A similar approach could apply to a division of sizeable court costs between litigants. That happened in unusual cross appeals by Clay and by a claimant on the other side of a controversy over land at the mouth of Green River, valued at $100,000. After he had been counsel in the case, the court appointed him the trustee to settle an involved estate. His opponent, Samuel Hopkins, had acquired only a parcel of it and now sued Clay for the way he executed the trust's terms. The judge was apparently so uncertain about this question that he ordered Clay and Hopkins to split the court costs.[18]

While his nonconstitutional cases often involved land, reflecting his special interest, there were, of course, other branches of his practice. A number concerned actions in debt during the early twenties, a period of hard times when debtors obtained judicial replevins, which postponed payment of obligations. Though Clay did not ordinarily favor such a policy, he represented some clients seeking such relief. Others were officials, such as sheriffs, arrayed against them. And in the early twenties he gave his principal attention to representing the national bank in Ohio and Kentucky in its massive effort to collect debts.

An interesting problem about a debt arose from its connection with Thomas Jefferson and lingered for several years. Clay received a letter from the aged ex-president, desperately urging him to sue a well-known Kentuckian, Thomas Owings, to collect an obligation of about $50,000. Jefferson and his grandson Thomas Mann Randolph had endorsed notes for Randolph's father-in-law, Wilson Cary Nicholas, in terrible financial shape when he died. Nicholas had transferred these notes as a loan to Owings, also out of pocket. Left with his commitment in the endorsement, Jefferson feared he would be ruined, hard-pressed as he had been and would increasingly become.

Clay agreed to take the case to the federal district court of Kentucky, where he eventually won a hollow victory. All he gained was the solace of an assignment of the worthless notes to another person. Despite the decision, Owings had been unable and unwilling to redeem them. Jefferson had not extricated himself from the financial depths and had been dead for several years.[19]

Rarely taking criminal cases, the lawyer did have a few. He felt obliged to take one at the urging of his longtime associate in law and politics Robert Wickliffe, who was a candidate for the state legislature in 1829. Wickliffe's opponent, John M. McCalla, had published a severe attack upon him anonymously in the Lexington *Kentucky Gazette*. Wickliffe's son, Charles, defended his father's reputation with more than a little zeal. He demanded that Thomas Benning, editor of the newspaper, reveal the author's name. A refusal to identify the writer as McCalla degenerated into a hot quarrel, which ended in young Wickliffe's shooting Benning dead and being charged with murder.

Clay hesitated to defend Charles, partly because of his long concentration on other branches of law but mainly because he recognized the damage it might cause him and his political friends to join such a rash foray. But he yielded to the elder Wickliffe's pleas as a necessity.

At the trial of five days, Clay displayed his oratorical skills by mimicking McCalla, a small man, by bending over to accentuate his short appearance, by speaking with a weak voice, and by asking the jury, according to an observer's account: "Who is Dentatus [the pseudonym used in the newspaper to attack Wickliffe]? Why, gentlemen, it is nobody but little Johnny McCalla!" Clay pictured Charles's act of shooting Benning as self-defense, a natural right of every person. Perhaps he made an impression with this point, since in his argument with Wickliffe, the editor had brandished his cane. That reaction could have been Benning's self-defense too. At any rate, the jury was out very briefly and returned a verdict of not guilty. Clay emerged with a good feeling about his success at the trial, as well as believing he had gained, not lost, politically. "I have greatly benefited by it, in this State," he said, "instead of being injuriously affected."

This did not conclude the ugly episode. Wickliffe challenged Benning's successor at the newspaper, George Trotter, to a duel after being called a murderer. This time, Charles lost. Trotter killed him. As a duelist himself, Clay did not dwell upon the bloody results of the controversy.[20]

Charles's brother, Robert Junior, was also short-tempered and involved in a dispute, leading to another criminal case. He clashed with Cassius Clay, Henry's distant relative, in an intraparty conflict of Whigs. The conservative Robert and the maverick Cassius had dueled but missed their shots—only the beginning of violent confrontation. Cassius continued to stir angry feelings because of his staunch antislavery advocacy. During the campaign of 1843, he repeatedly interrupted speeches of young Wickliffe, who resorted to another tactic to quiet this disagreeable nuisance by hiring a burly character, Sam Brown, to incite Cassius into a fight and to resort to a gun as needed. At a political gathering, Brown followed the plan and fired at Cassius, only to have the bullet harmlessly hit a metallic object on his adversary's chest. Whereupon Cassius spiritedly counterattacked with a knife he had handily brought along and cut up Brown rather badly. If someone, whether Cassius or Brown's friends, had not rolled Brown into the water of a nearby ravine, it was said, that would have been the last of him.

Cassius had survived, but he was indicted for committing the crime of mayhem. He brought in Henry Clay to defend him at his trial, notwithstanding Clay's earlier connections with the Wickliffes. In court, the lawyer relied upon self-defense as motive. He said Brown had aggressively called Cassius a liar to precipitate violence and had met a just response. For the state, the prosecutor blamed Cassius for instigating the encounter by hurling insults and flourishing a horse whip. According to later accounts of the trial, Clay's summation to the jury was eloquent and scathing, if not legalistic. His client could do no less than he did to repel aggression, he contended. A newspaper reporter quoted his concluding statement: "And, if he had not, he would not have been worthy of the name which he bears!" The attorney would not always take such pride in a connection with his volatile relative, Cassius Clay. But at the moment he was pleased with a verdict of innocence.[21]

Though Clay took the two Wickliffe criminal cases, they were exceptions to his primary interest as a lawyer. And at a time when others at the bar were handling much litigation on maritime issues, such as prizes, he had only one, *Apollon, Edon, Claimant* (1824) in the Supreme Court. He won damages from a federal collector's illegal seizure of a ship's cargo beyond the international boundary.[22] Another exception could have been the important subject of Indian rights, such as the cause of the Cherokees in Georgia, for whom he frequently expressed his support; however, he did not agree to defend their rights in prominent cases during the early thirties.[23]

Thus Clay's attention in nonconstitutional business usually went to questions about land or debt, areas where he was quite competent, as well as likely to collect sizeable fees. Americans were acquiring land by purchase, free-wheeling settlement, or inheritance. And with the land came uncertainties of title and location. The law regulating all this real estate was often similarly uncertain. Lawyers like Clay, in handling questions on land, drew upon the common law in English treatises, a few judicial reports, and scattered legislation. But this ancient body of law going back to feudalism needed to be balanced with new perspectives in a republican society.

As some of Clay's cases illustrate, courts sometimes tipped the balance in favor of ancient principles. In *McConnell* (1812), for example, the Kentucky Court of Appeals held for the inheritors of a large parcel of land because their right to the property rested upon the old Virginia requirement of primogeniture, in effect at the time of a will and applied at this late date. The same kind of dependence on ancient principles characterized *Kirk v Smith* (1824) in the Supreme Court. Clay and Webster, as counsel for Kirk, unsuccessfully challenged the long established proprietary interest of the Penn family in manors. Chief Justice Marshall's opinion for the Court respected remnants of William Penn's feudal right to quitrents, conferred a century and a half earlier. Similarly, the Court's decision in *New Orleans v De Armas and Cucullu* (1835) was another instance of an old legal interest thwarting modern challenges. In that case, Clay's clients, holding waterfront land by an ancient Spanish title in that city, prevailed against the municipal government's aim of occupying the land for new public facilities—notwithstanding the city's reliance upon the Louisiana Treaty of 1803 and a subsequent congressional law that transferred the territory to the United States. Chief Justice Marshall's ruling that the Court could not intervene not only confirmed old property rights of the defendants but specifically reflected Marshall's known reluctance for the Court to interfere in diplomatic policy.

While Clay continued to specialize in land questions, of course he had other types of business. There were some interesting and profitable cases involving wills. He earned sizeable fees in the protracted litigation concerning wills of his relatives, James and Ann Brown. It required stubborn but personally satisfying work. Still, his volunteer effort in behalf of the Singleton orphans to rescue a decision for their inheritance, was undoubtedly satisfying too. Then there were clients getting his help on problems of debt. A pitiful example was the sad situation of old Thomas Jefferson whose unwise financial obligations persisted even after his death.

Though he did not have unusual expertise in criminal law, Clay did take a few such cases. In his representation of the dueling young Wickliffes and his maverick relative, Cassius, Clay displayed the flashy techniques in addressing judge and jury he had developed in his younger years. His style of oratory and dramatic sense crowded out a more sober role in this setting. The result was less than perfect justice. But here, as in Clay's defense of Aaron Burr in the first stage of his treason trial, Clay was an able advocate.

In contrast to other lawyers, such as Webster, he did not have any noteworthy cases of maritime questions, perhaps because his home base was located in the interior of the country. Nevertheless, he did have more than a little preparation on this subject, gained from his diplomatic service after the War of 1812 and from his substantial experience as secretary of state in the twenties.

His contemporaries may have wondered why he did not participate in defense of the Cherokees, whose harsh treatment he deplored in and out of Congress. Even now, this is an appropriate question. Likewise, one can pose the same sort of question about his circumspection on problems of slavery as a lawyer.

6

∽

SLAVERY

Lawyers in antebellum America often addressed the rising question of slavery. Whether they were also active politicians or mainly lawyers, they encountered problems caused by the so-called peculiar institution. This was true of Clay. As politician, he faced congressional controversies about slavery in western territories and displayed an uncommon ability to forge national compromises. As lawyer in local and federal courts, he had professional business relating to slavery, and he showed his characteristic caution in handling it. The more so, because he was himself a large slaveholder.

During the final phase of his practice, the issue had reached a critical stage, threatening republican principles and the strength of the union. Not only confronting political crises, such as those about state power to nullify national legislation or about western expansion, Clay also struggled with sensitive legal issues about slavery.

That was the situation in *Groves v Slaughter* (1841), a case in the Supreme Court concerning the interstate slave trade.[1] People in Mississippi had become alarmed by a large importation of slaves for work in its extensive cotton fields. To members of a state constitutional convention in 1832, this traffic seemed to be dumping undesirable and dangerous workers from older states. There was a feeling, as well, that it drained capital from Mississippi. So the convention placed an article in the document prohibiting introduction of more slaves for sale after the coming year, though it did allow owners who were new settlers to bring their own slaves into the state. This constitution did not specify whether the article was self-enforcing or required subsequent action by the legislature. At any rate, that body did not enact a law on the subject until 1837.

Meanwhile in 1836 Robert Slaughter, an out-of-state trader, had exported a large number of slaves into Mississippi. In making the transaction, he received a promissory note, endorsed by Moses Groves, also a nonresident of the state. But a suit in the federal circuit court followed when Groves refused to pay on the note because, he reasoned, such sales were illegal according to the provision in the state constitution. Slaughter responded that the sale had been made before the legislature had passed a necessary statute in 1837 enforcing the prohibition. The state constitution on the point, he said, was not self-executing, so that his sale during the previous year was still legal. Groves, he contended, should pay on the endorsement. The federal court agreed. Whereupon, Groves appealed to the Supreme Court, with a hearing scheduled in the 1841 term.

Slaughter and a partner now asked Clay to represent them in what would turn out to be an intricate and important case, both economically and legally. In January, soon after the Log Cabin victory of his Whigs in the election of 1840, Clay was busy in the Senate preparing an agenda for the incoming Harrison administration. Yet he found time to take the case with a sizeable fee on the contingency of winning a judgment from the justices holding court down in the Capitol basement.[2]

On February 20, 1841, Robert Walker, a prominent states' rights Democrat, opened the hearing as counsel for Groves with a staunch defense of the state's policy prohibiting importation of slaves for sale. The most wicked and dangerous of them could contaminate the whole slave population, he warned. He also predicted trouble from agitators who would stir up discontent if the state were open to an unrestricted slave trade. Still another danger would follow judicial disapproval of the state's regulations: it would allow Congress to trample upon states' rights, dear to Walker's heart. Here he argued vigorously against application of the national commerce power to interfere with the state's internal affairs. His most persuasive point was a citation to many laws of other states, similar to those of Mississippi. In general, Walker's approach was exhaustive and his tone emotional. He later submitted a long written version to the court reporter, Richard Peters, who incorporated it as an appendix to the current volume of Supreme Court reports.[3]

Henry Gilpin also represented Groves and justified the state constitutional convention's provision as self-enforcing in prohibiting importation of slaves for sale. No matter that a statute had not been adopted before Slaughter's transaction. Here he conceded he had to rely upon common sense for this interpretation. He, too, rejected any use of the congressional power to regulate commerce as destructive of Mississippi's sovereignty over its domestic institutions. Interestingly, even fifty years after the adoption of the United States Constitution, Gilpin, the nation's attorney general, could expound concurrent state rather than broad federal regulation of interstate commerce. But in those days, that officer still had a private practice as well as duties for the national government. So Gilpin could express his own constitutional tenets of strict construction.[4]

Clay's longtime friend and veteran lawyer Walter Jones began argument for Slaughter. He insisted that the state constitutional article (1832) by itself, without an enforcing statute (none till 1837), was insufficient authority to prohibit Slaughter's slave sales (1836). And he was confident that when the statute was passed in 1837, it could not abrogate this earlier contract between Slaughter and Groves, for precedents of the Supreme Court on the contract clause of the United States Constitution prohibited state measures affecting agreements retrospectively. After a short presentation, Jones closed. He did not wish to dominate strategy for the defendant by crowding out his associates, Clay and Daniel Webster. He magnanimously remarked he would leave basic constitutional questions of the case to "the Ajax [Webster] and Achilles [Clay] of the bar."[5]

In his turn, Clay strengthened the objection to accepting the state constitutional article alone. If it were so accepted, he predicted, serious consequences would follow. Large numbers of slaves would be cast loose and would pose a serious threat to security, he warned. Nothing had been done to avoid this contingency, which might escalate to a "servile war." Legally, he believed the effect would be an unjust confiscation of a huge amount of slave owners' property. And it would be retrospective action, though he did not further develop the argument based upon the federal contract clause. Speaking from personal knowledge, however, he pointed out that the same kind of provision on importation of slaves in the Kentucky constitution had not allowed its operation in that state without appropriate legislation. The Mississippi legislature had finally done so, but after Slaughter's shipment.

As other counsel and some of the justices would do, Clay discussed the relevance of the constitutional power of Congress to regulate interstate commerce. Should the Court rule that the Mississippi policy interfered with it? He answered yes, for Congress had an "exclusive power." He did not elaborate this assertion by citing cases or exploring constitutional theory beyond an emphatic charge that the existing prohibition of importing slaves was on the "abolition side" of the question and confiscated a very important form of property. Anyway, he declared, abolition was not a legitimate regulation of commerce but an "annihilation" of it. Clearly, he would also not approve Congress's using its commerce power to weaken the right to conduct the interstate slave trade. He had elaborated that view in the Senate and would repeat it in the future.[6]

Aroused by the role of the Mississippi courts in approving the state's exclusion of slave imports, he directed an emotional blow against their competence—an interesting foray against the judicial system there in contrast to acceptable systems in this country generally. "Who are the judges of the Courts of Mississippi, and what is the tenure of their offices? They are elected by the people; and the judges so elected form the Court of Errors, and a Court thus constituted is called upon to decide a case affecting a large portion of the citizens of that state, in which strangers to the state, and those who have no influence in their appointment, are claimants! The judges of Mississippi are sitting in their own cause; in the cause of those around them; of those who gave and can take away their offices! . . . I hope never to live in a state where the judges are elected, and where the period for which they hold their offices is limited, so that elections are constantly recurring."[7]

Webster closed the argument for Slaughter by reiterating the point that the Mississippi constitutional article was not self-enforcing, only authorizing later legislative action. But he focused on the commerce clause of the federal Constitution. Like Clay, he subscribed to an exclusive congressional power, though not to interfere with the slave trade. He cited the steamboat-monopoly case of *Gibbons v Ogden* (1824) as ruling that Congress had complete power over commerce among the states, and they had none. If Congress did not legislate on a subject, it was meant to be free, he contended. According to this formula, only the subordinate and unclear police power for health and safety remained to the states, Webster said. However well-informed in constitutional law the lawyer was, he did not accurately describe the less extensive character of the *Gibbons* decision, which did not lay down an exclusive national commerce power. This despite his own important participation as counsel in that case. The division of the commerce power between national and state governments continued to be an open question. And the present disposition of *Groves* demonstrated it was.[8]

Another feature of the arguments of Clay and Webster was their description of slaves as property. While not a new concept in antebellum years, it was now gaining a broader significance. Slaves were a peculiar kind of property not to be arbitrarily seized or devalued by government. The state's denial of Slaughter's right to be protected from deprivation of his slave property was unconstitutional, the attorneys reasoned. Such an interpretation had developed from the "law of the land" clause in England's ancient Magna Carta, limiting royal power, later in state constitutions and the Fifth Amendment of the national Constitution, expressed as "due process of law." Justice Baldwin would employ that concept in his concurring opinion.

The Supreme Court splintered in its disposition of the case. Two justices out of the nine did not participate: John Catron was ill, and Philip Barbour had died before the decision. Two others, Joseph Story and John McKinley, did not file opinions but were listed by the Court reporter as dissenting. In an opinion for the Court, Smith Thompson therefore spoke for no more than a bare majority of five out of nine members. He took a restrained position by holding only that the Mississippi constitution was not self-executing and that the legislature had not enacted the necessary implementing statute to bar importation of slaves from other states. To that extent he held for Slaughter, Clay's client. He went no further and did not comment on other more fundamental questions, whether the state was invading congressional power over interstate commerce, whether it was depriving Slaughter of his property in slaves, or whether the Supreme Court was bound to follow the Mississippi state courts' decisions relevant to the present issues, indeed whether they were clearly formulated.[9] James Wayne was silent, but his proslavery sensitivity and disapproval of judicial intervention into the institution were well known. He gladly accepted Thompson's cautious approach. Henry Baldwin concurred but wrote a separate opinion with his own reasons, much bolder than Thompson's and resembling Clay's argument against the state's policy.[10] Roger Taney was stirred to rebuff strong statements by Baldwin and John McLean for a broad congressional commerce power. Otherwise, he approved Thompson's guarded strategy.[11]

Although Clay won his case, the decision was narrow and unclear. No more than one justice, probably Wayne, concurred entirely with Thompson's opinion, which therefore invited disagreement and noncompliance in the state. And that is exactly what happened. The Mississippi Court of Appeals had already held that the state constitution was self-enforcing and persisted in disputing *Groves* over the next several years. During argument in the case, Webster had urged the Supreme Court in vain to give no weight to such state decisions on this subject because they were not only premature but exceeded their jurisdiction.[12]

Finally in *Rowan v Runnels* (1847), the Supreme Court, speaking through Taney, did repel this opposition to its authority. He rejected an effort by the state judiciary to bypass the *Groves* ruling.[13] Dissatisfaction in Mississippi about the inflow of slaves continued for some time. Slaves, such as those marketed by Slaughter, were brought into the state for sale in large numbers in defiance of several state laws. Still, debts due to slave traders like Slaughter were often not paid. There must have been a feeling of futility by people on both sides of this controversy.

Groves had an untidy impact upon issues about slavery. Some justices supported national power to check its spread, and others opposed it. In this sense, the case ventilated a significant question in antebellum politics. While the legal status of slaves as property was becoming more important, there was here an early suggestion that the constitutional concept of due process of law was relevant. Later it was indeed relevant in the *Dred Scott* decision of 1857.[14]

More to the point, in *Groves* the Court explored how far and where the constitutional power to regulate commerce extended. Thompson's official opinion evaded a direct answer to this basic question. The other justices scattered: Story and McLean for an exclusive national power; Taney for state concurrent authority; and others for partial regulation at the two levels. Lawyers also differed—Webster for national and Walker for state power, others somewhere in between. So if *Groves* seemed to be chiefly a slavery case, it was also a highlight in the lively debate about commercial regulation. This development would reach a tentative resolution ten years later in the judicial compromise of

Cooley v Wardens (1851), allowing state concurrent regulation of some branches of interstate commerce but asserting exclusive national power over others found to be important "higher branches."[15]

Despite Clay's argument in *Groves* for extensive congressional power over interstate commerce, he conceded Congress could not interfere with intrastate commerce in slaves. And several years earlier in the Senate, he had denied favoring any national legislation restricting either level of slave trading, federal or state. In presenting a series of proslavery resolutions, John Calhoun had charged that Clay approved such regulations. The Kentuckian responded with his own resolutions setting forth a categorical disclaimer: "The Constitution provides no power to prohibit the slave trade or movement of slaves within and between slave-holding states."[16] Though Clay's resolutions did not pass, general sentiment in this period probably opposed any regulation of the interstate slave trade.

There were more exchanges on the subject, one of which occurred immediately after the *Groves* decision of 1841. In the lame-duck days before the new Harrison administration took office, Webster, who had been appointed secretary of state, sent the Senate his resignation as a member. An inveterate opponent, Alfred Cuthbert, who was quite upset but not well informed about the *Groves* hearing, rose to deplore Webster's absence from the chamber. He demanded that the lawyer explain to the Senate his negative views on states' rights and slavery, which Cuthbert believed would now detract from his fitness for the cabinet appointment. As a fellow Whig and co-counsel with Webster in *Groves,* Clay disputed this indictment by warmly insisting neither he nor Webster had ever subscribed to federal intervention in this area of states' rights. He even took the further step of saying he thought Congress had the positive power to remove obstacles to the movement of slaves across state lines.[17]

The problem arising from Slaughter's slave trading did not disappear. Up to the outbreak of the Civil War, this aspect of slavery was a target of abolitionists and non-extensionists despite whatever the Supreme Court said. Free Soilers and Republicans sought to stop slave trading as a blot on the national character that ought not be tolerated, and they believed it could be done constitutionally. This inflamed the southern "slave power" as an insupportable and illegal assault against its "peculiar institution." Supreme Court decisions and northern compromisers could not calm the alarm spreading across the South. The political direction the issues of the *Groves* case would finally take remained to be seen. At the moment, that direction seemed to favor the slavery interest.[18]

Though now a compromiser, carefully addressing the question of slavery in this stage of his political career, Clay had taken a stronger stand on it as a young man in frontier Kentucky. He had then sought but failed to get adoption of a policy of gradual emancipation to be inserted in the state constitution. Later, as president of the American Colonization Society, he confirmed his long-time association with the policy of removal to Africa. Now in arguing *Groves* he demonstrated his retreat from serious reform, politically and constitutionally.

7

∽

OVERVIEW

Clay's experience in the world of lawyers and judges extended from his apprenticeship as a boy of fourteen with the learned Chancellor George Wythe, then with state Attorney General Robert Brooke in Richmond, Virginia, and through a very long practice until his death more than fifty years later. Contrary to a common misconception about Clay's preparation as a lawyer, it was quite good in the circumstances. And after his admission to the Kentucky bar in 1798 until his death in 1852, he blended an active business in court with a long involvement in politics. He competed well with opposing counsel in grasp of fundamentals without excessive reliance upon his oratorical skills.[1] His correspondence and the court reports show close attention to factual details and a sure understanding of broad issues. Furthermore, Clay became one of the most important political figures of those decades, combining dual roles in law and public affairs. Each affected the other.

Energy and ambition, as well as a fortunate setting in the thriving western town of Lexington, helped him rise socially as a member of the prominent Hart family and advance professionally. Always a spur to his practice of law was his strong interest in fees he could collect, frequently in property in addition to cash, evident in his sizeable holdings of real estate, town lots and buildings, but particularly huge chunks of frontier land.

True enough, there were periods of little or no business in the courts, usually due to his political commitments. And when he returned to the bar, his feelings were guarded about reentry. There were moments when he looked back upon his early preparation as being limited. Still, these were passing exceptions in his own views about a professional career.[2] And certainly one does not find evidence that his contemporaries had anything but ample respect for his ability as a lawyer.

Clay's expertise in land law developed rapidly and never declined. Legal business in Kentucky and other western areas was brisk and complicated. Questions about titles, sales, and wills were quite challenging because early surveying and record keeping had been careless or nonexistent. If a lawyer was knowledgeable about this blurred subject, however, he could succeed and profit well indeed.

An important constitutional case, *Green v Biddle* (1824), illustrates the problem. Occupants of large areas of Kentucky had inadequate proof of land ownership, claimed by absentee Virginians who relied upon old grants issued wholesale by their legislature when Kentucky had been its western county. Later, Kentucky passed laws to protect and compensate the occupants, but Virginia persisted in supporting its claimants, so that the two states were arrayed against each other. Clay's effort for a political compromise met the Old Dominion's rebuff. And he lost in his resort to the Supreme Court, though another case finally allowed some relief from absentee claims. Nevertheless, *Green* had inflamed Clay and his friends, who strongly objected to this extension of the Constitution's contract clause to monitor interstate agreements judicially. Nowadays, a different procedure for state compacts prevails.

Additional land cases required detailed preparation. *Kirk v Smith* (1824) depended on the relevance of William Penn's original proprietary rights in Pennsylvania, and *Livingston v Story*

(1835–37) concerned land along the New Orleans levee, held by his longtime Democratic adversary Edward Livingston. Though the lawyer showed a sure grasp of land law, he lost both decisions. In *Kirk* the Supreme Court upheld old proprietary rights. In *Livingston* it allowed the common-law judicial procedure of equity relief instead of the civil code of Louisiana, upon which Clay had relied. He argued many other land questions, most of them nonconstitutional, in which federal and state tribunals inclined toward antiquated authorities in behalf of vested rights but for free enterprise as well. That was true of those in which Chief Justice Marshall delivered majority opinions.

A significant case defining the contract clause was *Odgen v Saunders* (1824–27). Interpreting the Constitution's provision that prohibits states from impairing the obligation of contracts (article 1, section 10), the justices applied it against retrospective bankruptcy laws but approved legislation on future contracts. In a very important second hearing they disapproved interstate extension of a state's measure on bankruptcy. This condition reduced state action and protected a developing national economy.

Clay uncharacteristically argued *Ogden* on the side of state power. He probably took the case because he and others in Congress had not yet succeeded in passing a national bankruptcy statute. So despite his firm nationalism, he urged desirable state action to fill a void in the sphere of economic growth. Though Marshall filed a rare dissent, even arguing against a partial state power, the Court did move the contract clause toward the later broad versions of constitutional due-process clauses, which would be invoked against legislation, state or national, retrospective or prospective. As for bankruptcy policy, with brief exceptions Clay's hopes for national laws were not fulfilled through the nineteenth century.

As a lawyer-politician, he had a great interest in banking. When he first became active in public affairs of Kentucky, he had much to do with the state banks there, in fact by serving as an officer and a counsel of these institutions. In Congress he did display his early version of Jeffersonianism by opposing rechar-

ter of the Bank of the United States in 1811, but he soon changed
his mind during the surge of nationalism after 1815. And from
that time forward he was one of the staunchest advocates of national banking. This position was reflected in congressional politics and in his personal dependence upon the bank for loans.
Still, he could later gain more constitutional room for state banks
too in winning *Briscoe v Kentucky* (1837), in which he also had
a personal interest. As an attorney for the BUS in the 1820s, he
supervised collection of debts in Ohio and Kentucky, which involved going into courts constantly for judicial executions of fore-
closure, successfully in nearly all instances but not necessarily
resulting in timely collections.

The negative effects upon opinion toward this corporation
in Ohio led into the well-known case of *Osborn v BUS* (1824).
Clay organized and implemented the legal strategy to get judgment against an Ohio tax, intended to force the bank out of that
state; and in the process he got a lower federal court ruling that
this was a suit against an individual official, Ralph Osborn, not
against the state of Ohio, which had claimed protection of the
Eleventh Amendment as a version of its sovereign immunity. From
here the question proceeded to the Supreme Court, where Chief
Justice Marshall affirmed the circuit court's holding for the bank.
The precedent of *Osborn* would be a possible but not sure weapon
against states in the future. Public policy might be overturned by
suit nominally against an official but actually against a state. Yet
the dividing line now, as in Clay's time, is fuzzy. Almost as a
matter of course, Marshall reiterated his classic pronouncement
in *McCulloch v Maryland* (1819) that the bank was both necessary and constitutional. Obviously, Clay's victory here did not
persuade anti-bank Jacksonian politicians in the future to accept
the existence and utility of a national bank.

Like some of his cases on banking and land, another subject
involving the relation of law and politics was slavery, demonstrated in *Groves v Slaughter* (1841). The circumstances surround-
ing this controversy developed in an effort by Mississippi to close
off the importation of slaves from other states. Robert Slaughter

defied that policy and retained Clay and Webster in his appeal to
the Supreme Court. Technically, the two lawyers argued that the
state's constitutional provision forbidding slave imports was in-
operable without enforcing legislation. And that was the point
accepted by the majority opinion. But more significant were other
arguments of counsel and opinions of several justices, ranging
across broader issues, however nonessential they were to dispos-
ing of the case before them. Both Clay and Webster contended
interstate commerce in slaves was constitutionally immune from
both state and national interference. States could not prohibit it
because the regulation of interstate commerce was an exclusive
national power, they ventured to say, while Congress could not
prohibit it because doing so would be an unconstitutional deprivation of a special kind of property. But the two lawyers could
not recruit a united opinion from the bench on these points.
Nonetheless, *Slaughter* was a revealing exploration of the constitutional options concerning slavery at a time it had become a
crucial question.

Exceptions to the economic questions that Clay emphasized
as a lawyer were a much smaller number of criminal cases. Occasionally during his early years, he represented persons accused of
assault or murder. In his usual role as defense attorney, he seemed
to depend a good deal upon his striking presence, his wit and
eloquence. And he might have carried the jury further than the
facts or the law justified in winning a verdict for a guilty client.
That was probably true of his defense of young Charles Wickliffe
and of Cassius Clay in the final phase of his practice.

By far, his best known criminal case had been to represent
Aaron Burr in the lower federal court's hearings on charges of
treason. At first, utterly convinced of Burr's innocence, Clay allowed his own personal feelings to get the better of him. He looked
at the prosecution as a Federalist attack upon this prominent
Republican. Nevertheless, he could not be faulted for successfully insisting on fair procedure by the grand jury. Aside from his
gullibility about Burr's character, he was on good ground with
respect to the constitutional rights of the accused. But Clay's readi-

ness afterward in Washington to fall immediately in line with President Jefferson's biased management of the Burr trial for treason was also influenced by politics beyond sober legal principles.

Clay had been more or less active in the practice of law over a long while, with some diversions when his political commitments prevented it, such as during the War of 1812 and its aftermath when congressional and diplomatic service absorbed his attention, or later when he served as John Quincy Adams's secretary of state in the late twenties. Otherwise he regularly traveled to Washington to appear before the Supreme Court and also to serve in Congress, besides conducting business in state tribunals.

Well known as he was throughout the country, it was not surprising for him to receive earnest requests from young persons to receive his instruction in the law. He regretfully declined but replied with lengthy advice about locating an office. He portrayed Kentucky, especially Lexington, as an ideal place to set up practice. Cincinnati and New Orleans were also strongly recommended. Obviously he demonstrated his own satisfaction in his past travel there.[3]

During these periods of nonappearance in courts, he probably misrepresented his situation, for when he was not prevented by other obligations, he returned to practice, despite leading his young correspondents to believe he might never return to the bar. At any rate, he took such occasions to offer extensive advice on professional and personal conduct.[4]

He also expressed his views to his son Henry Junior, who was uncertain about what direction he should take after graduation from the military academy at West Point. Clay favored a legal career decidedly and suggested a course of study for preparation and good locations to set up an office.[5] Young Henry took his father's counsel, though he later entered active military service and died during the Mexican War.

Even in the last months of his life in 1852 at age seventy-five when he lay dying in a Washington hotel room, Clay had some cases in progress. Too ill to appear in court, he had submitted briefs for other counsel to argue. In his last correspondence to his wife, he proudly reported he had received a fee of $2,500 in winning a suit in the Supreme Court, his reason for going to the capital. He remained quite interested in his remuneration, which had usually been liberal. Yet when he looked back upon his legal career, Clay could also feel satisfied with its character and quality during a formative era of American law.[6]

APPENDIX
TABLE OF CLAY'S CASES

Below are all cases for which Clay's arguments were officially reported in print. Asterisks indicate those he won. His numerous arguments of cases in county courts were not so reported. And though he participated in a number of federal circuit court cases, his arguments of them are not officially reported in the *Federal Cases*. Some cases with unreported arguments have been consulted.

U.S. SUPREME COURT

Skillern's Executors v May's Executors, 4 Cranch 137 (1807) and 6 Cranch 267 (1810)

Marshall v Currie, 4 Cranch 172 (1807)

Crockett v Lee, 7 Wheaton 522 (1822)*

Green v Biddle, 8 Wheaton 1 (1823)

Kirk v Smith, 9 Wheaton 241 (1824)

The Apollon, 9 Wheaton 362 (1824)*

Doddridge v Thompson, 9 Wheaton 469 (1824)*

Hughes v Edwards, 9 Wheaton 489 (1824)

Walton v U.S., 9 Wheaton 651 (1824)

Osborn v Bank of U.S., 9 Wheaton 738 (1824)*

Elmendorf v Taylor, 10 Wheaton 152 (1825)*

Ogden v Saunders, 12 Wheaton 213 (1827)*

Watts v Waddle, 6 Peters 389 (1832)*

Cincinnati v White's Lessee, 6 Peters 431 (1832)

Minor v Tillotson, 7 Peters 99 (1833)

Vattier v Hinde, 7 Peters 252 (1833)

Brown v Keene, 8 Peters 112 (1833)*

New Orleans v De Armas and Cucullu, 9 Peters 224 (1835)*

Life and Fire Insurance Company v Adams, 9 Peters 573 (1835)*

Livingston v Story, 9 Peters 632 (1835) and 11 Peters 351 (1837)

Boone v Chiles, 10 Peters 177 (1836)*

Briscoe v Bank of Kentucky, 11 Peters 257 (1837)*

Groves v Slaughter, 15 Peters 449 (1841)*

KENTUCKY APPELLATE COURT

Hickman v Boffman, 3 Kentucky 365 (1808)*

Bank of U.S. v Norton, 10 Kentucky 422 (1821)*

Clay v Hopkins and *Hopkins v Clay*, 10 Kentucky 485 (1821)*

Alexander v Leatch, 10 Kentucky 503 (1821)*

Lampton v Taylor, 16 Kentucky 273 (1821)*

Thomas ads Clarke, 11 Kentucky 287 (1821)*

Madison's Heirs v Owens, 16 Kentucky (1821)

McConnell v Brown, 16 Kentucky 459 (1821)

Sheriff and Baker v Seldon, 16 Kentucky 485 (1821)*

Bates v Todd's Heirs, 14 Kentucky 177 (1823)*

Singleton v Singleton, 47 Kentucky 340 (1847)*

NOTES

1. THE LEGAL SCENE

1. The foregoing discussion on legal issues in Kentucky draws upon the valuable treatment in Ellis, *Jeffersonian Crisis*, 111–57.

2. Baxter, *Daniel Webster*, passim.

3. White, *Marshall Court*, 201–383; *Hickman v Boffman*, 3 Kentucky 365–73.

4. Johnson, *Chief Justiceship of John Marshall*; White, *Marshall Court*, 292–383.

5. Newmyer, *Supreme Court Justice Joseph Story*.

6. Smith, *John Marshall*, 502–3; Marshall to Clay, Nov. 28, 1828, in Hopkins, et al., eds., *The Papers of Henry Clay*, 7:550–51. *The Papers of Henry Clay* is cited below as CP.

7. White, *Marshall Court*, 746, 978–79.

8. Clay's only maritime case in the Supreme Court was *Apollon, Eden, Claimant*, 9 Wheaton 362 (1824).

9. 2 Wheaton 206 (1817).

10. White, *Marshall Court*, 9–11, 49, 76–157.

11. Mushkat and Rayback, *Martin Van Buren*, 18–61 and passim.

12. Baxter, *Henry Clay*, 199–210.

13. Frank, *Lincoln as a Lawyer*, 78–173.

14. Holt, *Political Crisis*, 4–8, 16–19, 258.

15. White, *Marshall Court*, 9–11.

16. Ibid., 61–156.
17. *Livingston v Story,* 11 Peters 351 (1837).
18. Nelson, *Americanization of the Common Law,* 145–65.
19. 11 Peters 351–419 (1837).
20. On this subject and others on legal history, the most informative reference is Lawrence M. Friedman, *History of American Law.*

2. EARLY PRACTICE

1. Remini, *Henry Clay,* 1–8.
2. Ibid., 9–13; Van Deusen, *Life of Henry Clay,* 3–15; Mayo, *Henry Clay,* 20–25.
3. *CP,* 1:2–3.
4. Van Deusen, *Life of Henry Clay,* 18–19.
5. Clay published a letter in the *Kentucky Gazette* on Apr. 25, 1798, signed "Scaevola," urging legislative authority for voluntary emancipation and emphasizing the injustice of slavery. He served as president of the Colonization Society during much of his later years. *CP,* 1:4–6. His bold advocacy of a constitutional amendment at this early age demonstrates his self-confidence as a lawyer as well as a reformer critical of slave labor.
6. Remini, *Henry Clay,* 17–31.
7. See Clay's memorandum on the court system in *CP, Supplement,* 57; Mayo, *Henry Clay,* 96 and passim.
8. Agreement of Clay with Peacock Wrenshall & Company of Pittsburgh, Sept. 24, 1804, *CP,* 1:150–51; Luke Tiernan & Co. of Baltimore to Clay, Jan. 30, 1808, ibid., 18–19; James Smith, Jr., of Philadelphia to Clay, Nov. 16 and 23, Dec. 26, 1810, ibid., 501–5.
9. Clay to Taylor, Dec. 2, 1800, *CP, Supplement,* 2–6; and June 1, 1802, *CP,* 1:81. There are numerous letters from Clay to Taylor on collecting debts as late as 1808 in the supplement.
10. Clay to Taylor, Nov. 1, 1799, *CP, Supplement,* 1.
11. Ibid., 3.
12. Clay's statement of transactions and of payments to him, [Apr. 5, 1803], *CP,* 1:105–8. For his services from 1800 to 1803, he received $7,764.29. See the table of cases, including those that relate to debt collections during the periods of representing Taylor. Those in the Kentucky appellate court and the federal Supreme Court were reported in print and therefore show more detail than those in the county courts not in print.

13. A revealing comment on the difficulty of identifying boundaries of land claims is Clay's opinion of Feb. 23, 1804, on the subject. It identified them in terms of creeks and trees, but with emphasis upon the general "notoriety" of the plot—obviously a flexible standard. Ibid., 131–32.

14. Thomas Norvell to Clay, [Dec. 13, 1800], ibid., 4–44.

15. Editorial note, ibid., 22–23, lists the cases, most of them in the Fayette County Court. One, *Frazier v Steel*, which Clay won, was decided by the Kentucky Court of Appeals in 1804 and reported in 2 Kentucky 334–54.

16. *Marshall v Currie*, 4 Cranch 172–77 (1807). At this term of the Supreme Court, Clay also argued another case involving 2,500 acres of land in Kentucky, entangled by faulty procedures in early grants, typical of the times. The postponed decision ordered a partition of the disputed tract between the parties. *Skillern's Executors v May's Executors*, 4 Cranch 137–41 (1807) and 6 Cranch 267–68 (1810).

17. 3 Kentucky 356–73 (1808). An interesting sidelight of Clay's argument was the court's rejection of his effort to cite an English case on the ground that a state statute prohibited acceptance of such precedents. Clay had opposed adoption of that measure when he was a member of the legislature.

18. Colton, ed., *Life, Correspondence, and Speeches*, 1:79.

19. Texts of Agreements, *CP,* 1:46–47, 52, 60.

20. Tax bill for 1808 (Feb. 10, 1809), ibid., 402. Figures for 1811, ibid., 526; and for 1812, ibid., 628.

21. Ibid., 14 and 58.

22. Brown to Clay, ibid., 27; Sargent, *Life and Public Services*, 17–18.

23. Van Deusen, *Life of Henry Clay,* 27; Sargent, *Life and Public Services,* 17–18.

24. Colton, ed., *Life, Correspondence, and Speeches,* 1:85–86.

25. Ibid., 96.

26. Eaton, *Henry Clay,* 13.

27. Prentice, *Biography of Henry Clay,* 18–19.

28. Among many references describing the so-called Burr conspiracy, those most useful on Clay's role in the story are Mayo, *Henry Clay,* 222–70; McCaleb, *Aaron Burr Conspiracy*; Abernethy, *Burr Conspiracy*; and Remini, *Henry Clay,* 41–46. McCaleb concludes Burr did not commit treason, while Abernethy finds evidence of guilty conspiracy.

29. Mayo, *Henry Clay,* 222–32.

30. After failing to rouse Jefferson, as well as Madison, Daveiss

had his correspondence published in a pamphlet released by Joseph Street, an editor of a Frankfort newspaper. A reprint is available in "A View of the President's Conduct Concerning the Conspiracy of 1806," ed. Cox and Swineford, *Quarterly Publications of the Historical and Philosophical Society of Ohio* 12 (1917):58–154.

31. See 25 *Federal Cases* 1–2 (1806) for text of Daveiss's motion in federal circuit court of Kentucky. Report of further hearings is in ibid., 19–20. More information is in Wilson, ed., "The Court Proceedings of 1806 in Kentucky against Aaron Burr and John Adair." The following discussion of judicial proceedings on the Burr case in Kentucky draws from these sources. See also Jillson, "Clay's Defense," 1–8.

32. Ibid.

33. Burr to Clay, Nov. 27, 1806, *CP*, 1:13.

34. Burr to Clay, Dec. 1, 1806, ibid., 14.

35. *CP*, 1:258–69.

36. Mayo, *Henry Clay*, 252–55.

37. Some time after the end of the Burr controversy, Clay quarreled with an aggressive critic, who attacked his mode of defending Burr, including opposition to Daveiss's attempt to guide the grand jury's deliberations. Clay assumed the pseudonym of "Regulus." The lively exchange was published by the critic in the *Lexington Reporter* and by Clay in the *Kentucky Gazette* during May into July, 1808. It is reprinted with editorial notes in *CP*, 1:328–43, 346–53, 358–60.

38. Ibid., 255–60.

39. Lomask, *Aaron Burr*, 2:118–22. Lomask cites a recent editorial analysis of the documents in the Burr manuscripts.

40. Abernethy, *Burr Conspiracy*, 190–91.

41. Clay to Thomas Hart, Feb. 1, 1807, *CP*, 1:273–74. In a conversation with William Plumer in Washington, Clay said he had not observed any illegal action by Burr's followers at Blennerhasset's island in Ohio on the way to the capital. This comment preceded Clay's call upon the president, who obviously changed the new senator's opinion about Burr's plan. Editorial note, ibid., 1:274–75. Clay did not sense any disapproval in Washington concerning the role of either Judge Innes or himself as Burr's counsel in proceedings of the court in Kentucky. Clay to Thomas Todd, Jan. 24, 1807, ibid., 272.

42. Clay to Caesar Rodney, Dec. 5, 1807, *CP*, 1:310–11.

43. Clay to Lewis Sanders, Apr. 26, 1807, and editorial note, *CP*, 1:290–91; Clay's "Argument Relative to Harman Blennerhassett," [July

15, 1807], ibid., 300–301; Remini, *Henry Clay*, 51; Nathan Schachner, *Aaron Burr*, 425–26.

44. Wickliffe to Clay, Jan. 9, 1811, *CP*, 1:616–17. Other correspondence about legal work Wickliffe handled for him at this time is in ibid., passim.

45. Mayo, *Henry Clay*, 94–95, based upon unpublished records of cases.

46. Clay himself contributed to that view by often expressing his regret in not applying himself more seriously to the study of law in his early years. Actually, his preparation under Wythe and Brooke, as well as his contacts with gifted persons of bar and bench in Richmond, placed him well above the average of his day.

47. Remini, *Henry Clay*, 32.

48. Clay's proposed resolution in the state legislature for expanding the federal court system, Dec. 17, 1804, *CP*, 1:163. His bill in the national Senate, Jan. 14, 1807, passed on Feb. 24, 1807. *U.S. Statutes at Large*, 2:420–21.

49. Clay to John Breckinridge, Dec. 22, 1804, *CP*, 1:166–67.

50. See above, n. 18, for *Hickman v Boffman*, 3 Kentucky 356–73 (1808).

51. Clay to John Breckinridge, Dec. 22, 1804, *CP*, 1:166–67.

3. ECONOMIC ISSUES

1. Connelly and Colter, *History of Kentucky*, 2:650–55.

2. Ibid., 655–58. See a study of the *Green* case described by Van Burkleo in *Oxford Companion to the Supreme Court of the United States* (New York, 1992), 146–47.

3. *Session Laws of Kentucky*, Feb. 17, 1797, and Jan. 27, 1812. Horwitz, *Transformation of American Law*, 56–61, describes the legal policy of a number of states, similar to that of Kentucky, and refers to relevant judicial cases.

4. *Kentucky Statutes* (Louisville, 1894), 43–45.

5. Jillson, *The Kentucky Land Grants*. John Green is listed for 10,000 acres, mostly in Fayette County. Richard Biddle is not listed. Clay is listed for several tracts.

6. Humphrey Marshall, brother-in-law of Chief Justice John Marshall, held 97,000 acres and had been an official surveyor of lands.

Thomas Marshall, a brother of John, held 128,000. Editorial note, *CP,* 3:756–58.

7. There is no report of the Supreme Court's proceedings in the volume for 1821, but there is for 1821 as well as 1823 after a second hearing. See 8 Wheaton 108 (1823) and the discussion below for the first hearing. For an informative comment on the procedure of amicus curiae, see Justice Sandra Day O'Connor, "Henry Clay and the Supreme Court," *The Register of the Kentucky Historical Society* 94 (Autumn 1996): 353–62, remarking that this procedure was novel in *Green,* but nowadays is frequently used in the Court.

8. Text of Clay's address to the Virginia legislature, Feb.7, 1822, *CP,* 3:161–70.

9. Ibid., 176, and editorial note, 177.

10. Ibid., 176–77, 207–8, 215–18. An important reason for Virginia's rejection was its dissatisfaction with Kentucky's reluctance to recognize many claims of Virginians to extensive lands in western Kentucky, based upon Old Dominion warrants for their military service. If Kentucky had been more accommodating on this issue, there might have been some sort of compromise by the two states on the land-occupant question. Clay spent a great deal of time arranging appointments of commissioners to arbitrate the disputes. That effort collapsed.

11. Ibid., 387.

12. Marshall and members of his family had been active in holding land in Kentucky for a long time, but he did not participate in the case and had transferred this property to relatives. However, his influence on other members of the Court could have been a factor in the outcome. Johnson, *Chief Justiceship of John Marshall,* 78.

13. 8 Wheaton 1–18 (1823). For reactions to the first hearing and movement toward the second, see editorial note, *CP,* 3:91; William Duval to Clay, ibid., 89–91; Governor John Adair's message to the Kentucky legislature, Oct. 16, 1821, *Niles' Weekly Register,* Nov.17, 1821; Richard Biddle to Clay, Oct. 24 and 25, *CP,* 3:341–44.

14. 8 Wheaton 18–31, 58–69 (1823).

15. Ibid., 39–56.

16. Ibid., 57–58.

17. Ibid., 69–94.

18. Ibid., 94–107.

19. *Niles' Weekly Register,* Nov. 29, 1823.

20. Ibid., Dec. 27, 1823.

21. Clay to Benjamin W. Leigh, Dec. 22, 1823, *CP,* 3:550.

22. Clay to Francis Brooke, Mar. 9, 1823, ibid., 392. The report of the debate in Congress, showing reaction to the *Green* decision, is in *Annals of Congress*, 18:1 (1823), 2514–620. In *Briscoe v Bank of Kentucky*, 11 Peters 257 (1837), Marshall was later reported to have said that "the practice of this court is not (except in cases of absolute necessity) to deliver any judgment where constitutional questions are involved, unless four judges concur in opinion, thus making the decision that of the whole court."

23. Adams, *Memoirs*, 6:138.

24. Clay to Francis Brooke, Aug. 28, 1823, *CP*, 3:478–79.

25. Speech in Congress, Mar. 13, 1818, *CP*, 2:472–73; Clay to Francis Biddle, Aug. 7, 1824, ibid., 3:805.

26. Beveridge, *Life of John Marshall*, 4:371–75; Warren, *Supreme Court*, 1:652–63.

27. *Annals of Congress*, 18 Cong., 1 sess., 2514–620.

28. Clay to Benjamin W. Leigh, July 31, 1824, *CP*, 3:802–3; editorial note, ibid., 803.

29. *Bodley v Gaither*, 19 Kentucky 57–59 (1825).

30. 5 Peters 457 (1831).

31. U.S. Constitution, art. 1, sec. 10, par. 1: "No State shall . . . pass any . . . Law impairing the Obligation of Contracts."

32. U.S. Constitution, art. 1, sec. 10, par. 3: "No State shall, without the consent of Congress, . . . enter into any Agreement or Compact with another State."

33. Frankfurter and Landis, "The Compact Clause of the Constitution." This comprehensive, authoritative article shows that the compact clause and not the contract clause has been the provision applying to interstate agreements.

34. A search of historians' interpretations of the *Green* case shows little criticism of the Court's application of the contract clause to interstate relations. But a convincing view comes from Benjamin Wright in *Contract Clause of the Constitution*, 46–47. He says the decision was "perhaps the most far-fetched" extension of the contract clause. White, *Marshall Court*, 76, is also an exception to most references. He concludes the contract clause, rather than the compact clause, was "erroneously" applied.

35. 12 Wheaton 213–369 (1827). Sanders's name was often misspelled as Saunders, as it is in the Supreme Court reports.

36. 4 Wheaton 122 (1819). The constitutional basis for *Sturges* was art. 1, sec. 10, forbidding a state law that impairs the obligation of

contracts. For the hearings and opinions on *Sturges* and *Saunders,* see the description in Baxter, *Daniel Webster,* 110–19.

37. 12 Wheaton 226–37 (1827). The Court reporter combined the arguments of 1824 and 1827 by counsel of each side. Thus there were two hearings. Clay argued only in the first, in 1824.

38. Ibid., 237–54; Baxter, *Daniel Webster,* 112–19.

39. 12 Wheaton 237 (1827).

40. Ibid., 240; Konefsky and King, eds., *The Papers of Daniel Webster, Legal Papers.* Vol.3, *The Federal Practice,* ed. by King, pt. 1, 317–23. Clay received some advice from the chief justice of the Kentucky appellate court, John Boyle. Other information on this case is in this reference.

41. 12 Wheaton, 254–70 (1827).

42. Ibid., 271–92. An informative discussion of these bankruptcy cases is in White, *Marshall Court,* 648–56.

43. 12 Wheaton, 332–57 (1827).

44. Coleman, *Debtors and Creditors in America,* 269–93. See also Warren, *Bankruptcy in United States History.*

45. Coleman, *Debtors and Creditors in America,* 104, 127.

46. Baxter, *Henry Clay,* 169–70, 175–76.

47. 6 Howard 486 (1848).

48. *Stone v Farmers' Loan and Trust Co.,* 116 U.S. 307 (1886); *Munn v Illinois,* 94 U.S.113 (1877). Wright, *Contract Clause,* 94–178, is a good discussion of the relationship of the contract clause and the due process amendment.

4. BANKING

1. Clay's agreement with John Hart to form a mercantile company, providing that Clay would supply capital of $20,000, [Jan. 29, 1816], *CP,* 2:159–60. Mortgage deed of Lexington estate, Ashland, with bond executed to John Jacob Astor for $40,000, [Apr. 10, 1819], ibid., 685–87. Mortgage of Kentucky Hotel to Bank of the United States for $22,000, [July 8, 1820], ibid., 876–77.

2. *Reporter,* June 7, 1820, quoted in *CP,* 2:869.

3. Clay to Langdon Cheves, Nov. 5, 1820, ibid., 900–901.

4. Clay to Cheves, Feb. 10, 1821, ibid., 3:24–26; Cheves to Clay, Feb. 23, 1821, ibid., 47–48; and Mar. 3, 1821, ibid., 57–58; Clay to Cheves, June 23, 1822, ibid., 238. In his account book, Clay recorded

his income as $10,030 for the period of January 1822 to March 1823. Ibid., 3:402.

5. Clay to Cheves, Jan. 18, 1821, *CP, Supplement,* 83; Nicholas Biddle to Clay, Dec. 31, 1823, *CP,* 3:557; Clay to Biddle, Jan. 3, 1824, ibid., 558–60. Debts of the Johnsons to the BUS amounted to several hundred thousand dollars. The editorial note in *CP, Supplement,* 83, concludes that the bank came out of this financial problem well.

6. Clay to Cheves, Jan. 22, 1821, *CP,* 3:11–14. There are many items concerning Clay's work as a BUS lawyer in the early 1820s in *CP, Supplement.*

7. Clay to Gorham A. Worth, Dec. 12, 1820, *CP,* 2:909–10; Clay to Cheves, Feb. 27, ibid., 50–51; and Mar. 10, 1821, ibid., 3:63–66; Clay's circular letter to the bank's western offices on procedures, May 1, 1821, ibid., *Supplement,* 87–88.

8. Clay to George Jones, Oct. 7, 1822, ibid., 118–19.

9. Clay to George Jones, Nov. 21, 1822, ibid., 119–25.

10. 9 Peters 405–16 (1835); Clay to Langdon Cheves, June 16, 1822, *CP,* 3:228–34.

11. Clay to Cheves, ibid., 99.

12. Clay to Cheves, Jan. 12, 1822, ibid., 155.

13. Numerous instructions by Clay about these land cases have been published in *CP, Supplement.*

14. Clay to Cheves, Sept. 13, 1822, ibid., 286–87. Clay said he had obtained 211 favorable judgments for the Cincinnati branch alone.

15. Biddle to Clay, Jan. 25, 1823, ibid., 354–55, among other letters.

16. Charles Hammond to Clay, ibid., 3:245–46.

17. Stevens, "Clay, the Bank, and the West in 1824," 843–48.

18. Connelley and Coulter, *History of Kentucky,* 2:650–53; 4 Wheaton 316 (1819).

19. HC to Edmund W. Rootes, Nov. 24, 1818, *CP,* 2:605.

20. Ibid.; *Bank of the U.S. v Norton,* 10 Kentucky 422–29 (1821), reversing *Bank of the U.S. v Norvell,* 9 Kentucky 101–9 (1819).

21. 2 Federal Cases 728–33 (1822); Clay to Cheves, Nov. 14, 1819, *CP,* 2:723.

22. Clay to Nicholas Biddle, Dec. 27, 1822, *CP,* 3:347–48; the Kentucky Court of Appeals in *Blair v Williams,* decided that most of the relief laws were invalid because they were retrospective. *Niles' Weekly Register,* Nov. 8, 1823, and Jan. 3, 1824. Later the Supreme Court held that federal courts did not have to follow the procedural rules of Ken-

tucky courts, such as those affecting the judicial process against a debtor. *Wayman v Southard,* 10 Wheaton 1 (1825).

23. Clay to Cheves, Dec. 3, 1821, *CP,* 3:144.

24. Bogart, "Taxation of the Second Bank of the United States by Ohio"; Huntington, "A History of Banking and Currency in Ohio," 266–69, 283–91, 313–28.

25. Huntington, "A History of Banking and Currency in Ohio," 314–18.

26. Ibid., 319.

27. Ibid.

28. *Niles' Weekly Register,* Jan. 20, 1821; Clay to Cheves, Sept. 8, 1821, *CP,* 3:111–13; Clay's statement about proceedings of the federal circuit court, which appeared in the Washington *National Intelligencer* and was reprinted in *Niles' Weekly Register,* Sept. 29, 1821.

29. Text of the circuit court's opinion in *Niles' Weekly Register,* Sept. 9, 1820.

30. Text of Hammond's report in ibid., Jan. 20, 1821.

31. Ibid., Jan. 5, 1822, and Jan. 24 and 25, 1824; *Bank of U. S. v Planters' Bank,* 9 Wheaton 904 (1824).

32. *Niles' Weekly Register,* Feb. 23, 1822. Several states did express some support for Ohio: Indiana, Illinois, Tennessee, Pennsylvania, and Virginia. Beveridge, *Life of John Marshall,* 4:334.

33. *Niles' Weekly Register,* Oct. 30, 1819.

34. Clay to Cheves, Nov. 5, 1820, *CP,* 2:900–01.

35. Clay's resolution in the House, [Feb. 12, 1821], and editorial note, *CP,* 3:31.

36. Clay to George Jones et al., Aug. 6, 1821, *CP, Supplement,* 93–94.

37. Clay to Cheves, Jan. 22 and 31, 1821, *CP,* 3:13, 20–21.

38. Clay to Cheves, Feb. 15, 1821, ibid., 41.

39. Clay to Cheves, Oct. 22, 1821, ibid., 128–29; Nicholas Biddle to Clay, Feb. 4, 1823, *CP, Supplement,* 129–30.

40. 9 Wheaton 738–95 (1824).

41. Ibid., 795–811. See below for Marshall's opinion on this key point.

42. *U.S. v Peters,* 5 Cranch 115 (1809).

43. *Cohens v Virginia,* 6 Wheaton 264 (1821).

44. While argument of *Osborn* was in progress, Clay had referred to the *Roberts* case as a precedent in a letter of Feb. 17, 1824, to Nicho-

las Biddle. *CP*, 3:646–47. The report of *Bank of U.S. v Roberts* is in 2 Federal Cases 728–33 (1822).

45. *Osborn v Bank*, 9 Wheaton 816–71. Marshall also ruled against Georgia in its claim of sovereign immunity from suit for its partially owned state bank. He decided for the branch of the national bank. It was a step toward a more favorable legal status of interstate corporations. *Bank of U.S. v Planters' Bank*, 9 Wheaton 904 (1824).

46. *Osborn v Bank*, 871–903.

47. *Governor of Georgia v Madrazo*, 1 Peters 110 (1828).

48. *In re Ayers*, 123 U.S. 443 (1887); Currie, *The Constitution in the Supreme Court*, 102–8, 418–28.

49. Among the many references in legal history on the long-range question of sovereign immunity, the most useful is Jacobs, *The Eleventh Amendment and Sovereign Immunity*.

50. Clay's resolutions, [Oct. 18, 1820], *CP*, 2:895.

51. Clay's memorandum of his assets, including debts due him by the Bank of Kentucky, [Dec. 26, 1822], *CP*, 3:345–46; Clay's agreement with Bank of Kentucky, [Nov. 10, 1823], ibid., 519.

52. Clay to Nicholas Biddle, Dec. 6, 1823, ibid., 532–33; and also to Biddle, Dec. 22, ibid., 548–49.

53. Clay to Littleton D. Teackle, Jan. 24, 1825, ibid., 4:40.

54. The bank had lost an earlier case in the Kentucky county and appeals courts in *Lampton v Commonwealth's Bank*, 12 Kentucky 300–301 (1822) on a ruling that its notes were unconstitutional bills of credit. Now in the federal Supreme Court Briscoe was appealing another state decision, *Briscoe v Bank of Commonwealth*, 30 Kentucky 349 (1832), which had gone the other way, favorably for the Kentucky bank.

55. *Craig v Missouri*, 4 Peters 410 (1830). Reports of circuit court cases are in U.S. Supreme Court Records and Briefs for the period 1836–1838.

56. 11 Peters 257 (1837), headnote referring to the first hearing of the case in 1834, in which Clay did not appear as counsel.

57. Ibid., 263–75, 285–311.

58. Ibid., 280–85.

59. *Bank of Kentucky v Wister*, 2 Peters 318 (1828). The Supreme Court had, in fact, avoided holding state bank notes unconstitutional, but did so on narrow grounds of jurisdiction. So both sides in the present *Briscoe* case cited *Wister* to support their arguments.

60. 11 Peters 285 (1837).

61. Ibid.

62. Ibid., 328–50.

63. Newmyer, *Supreme Court Justice Joseph Story*, 222, criticizes the majority for acting "out of ignorance or politics or both." It was an abandonment of "scientific standards of adjudication," and an example of "judicial subjectivism," that upset Story, the author says. Ibid., 234. Currie, *The Constitution in the Supreme Court*, 207–8, convincingly praises Story for "sparkling scholarship" in defining bills of credit. Swisher, *History of the Supreme Court*, vol. 5, *Taney Period, 1836–64*, 107–9, does not take a strong interpretive position but provides a good narrative and explains the connection of the case with state bank notes. After looking into the large range of historical references, one can accept Story's interpretation of bills of credit as strictly constitutional but recognize the importance of state bank notes in this period. None of the viewpoints in the controversy was free of subjective politics.

64. In 1865 during extensive changes of wartime banking and currency, Congress taxed state bank notes out of circulation.

5. Nonconstitutional Business

1. White, *Marshall Court*, 747.

2. Ibid., 751–74; Friedman, *History of American Law*, 202–24. Some discussion of Clay's early land cases, including the *Green* case, is presented in chaps. 1 and 2 above.

3. 16 Kentucky 459–68 (1821); *CP*, 3:84–85.

4. 9 Wheaton 241–56 (1824).

5. Ibid., 256–325. This was typical of an increasing number of land cases handled by federal circuit courts on the basis of diversity of citizenship of the parties, not involving a federal question. There is a good discussion of the case and this trend in Johnson, *Chief Justiceship of John Marshall*.

6. Clay to Lucas Brodhead, Jan. 17, 1821, *CP, Supplement*, 82–83; and Mar. 8, 1823, ibid., 134; 10 Wheaton 154–81 (1825).

7. 9 Peters 632–36 (1835).

8. 9 Peters 640–42 (1835).

9. 11 Peters 351–419 (1837). White, *Marshall Court*, 855, says the Supreme Court had been allowing state courts to "exercise equity jurisdiction even where a state had no equity courts."

10. 9 Peters 224–39 (1835).

11. *Brown v Keene,* 8 Peters 112–17 (1833); *Preston v Keene,* 14 Peters 113–40 (1840); *Preston v Humphreys* (1844), in Louisiana Supreme Court. See Burns, "Henry Clay Visits New Orleans."

12. *Preston v Humphreys* in Louisiana Supreme Court, argued by Clay in 1844. The detailed litigation is described in Burns, "Henry Clay Visits New Orleans." The final phase was discussed in Clay's correspondence. Clay to Lucretia Clay, Jan. 28, 1843, *CP,* 9:800–01; Isaac T. Preston to Clay, Apr. 26, 1844, ibid., 10:10–11; and Clay to Preston, May 4, 1844, ibid., 10:50–51.

13. 47 Kentucky 340–77 (1847).

14. Duncan McArthur to Clay, Jan. 8, 1821, *CP,* 3:7–8; Clay to McArthur, Jan. 26, 1821, ibid., 16; 9 Wheaton 469–83. Counsel's arguments were not reported.

15. Thomas Hinde to Clay, [Jan. 6, 1821]. The case was first heard in the federal circuit court of Ohio but the two judges were divided, sending it on appeal to the Supreme Court. Clay did not participate in the hearing there. 7 Wheaton 23–27 (1822).

16. 6 Peters 389 (1832). Afer the case had hobbled along for sixteen years, the parties were understandably ready for an accommodation.

17. 14 Kentucky 177–86. The reporter commented in a headnote that the outcome was a compromise, though the amounts allowed were "disproportionate."

18. *Clay v Hopkins* and *Hopkins v Clay,* 10 Kentucky 485–89.

19. Jefferson to Clay, Aug. 28, 1823, and editorial note, *CP,* 3:280–81, citing Jefferson papers in the Library of Congress.

20. Clay's correspondence in 1829 about the case of young Charles Wickliffe, as well as editorial notes, are useful on this subject. *CP,* 8, passim. The standard source is Calvin Colton, ed., *Life, Correspondence, and Speeches,* 1:90–93. Colton was Clay's friend and early biographer. A scholarly reference is Dwight Mikkelson, "The *Kentucky Gazette,* 1787–1848."

21. Smiley, *Lion of White Hall,* 60–64; Cassius Clay, *Life of Cassius Marcellus Clay,* 71–89.

22. 9 Wheaton 362–80 (1824); editorial note about the case in *CP,* 3:397–98.

23. Ann Garram et al. to Clay, editorial note, *CP,* 8:165.

6. SLAVERY

1. 15 Peters 449 (1841).
2. Editorial note, *CP*, 9:475–76, is useful for the background of the case.
3. 15 Peters 1–88 and appendix, i-lxxxv (1841).
4. Ibid., 452–76.
5. Ibid., 476–81.
6. Ibid., 481.
7. Ibid., 481–89.
8. Ibid., 489–503; Baxter, *Daniel Webster,* 209–11.
9. 15 Peters 496–503 (1841).
10. Ibid., 510–17.
11. McLean's opinion, ibid., 503–8; Baldwin's opinion, ibid., 510–17.
12. Catterall, ed., *Judicial Cases Concerning American Slavery,* 3:278–89, describes cases in the Mississippi courts.
13. 5 Howard 134 (1847).
14. *Dred Scott v Sandford,* 19 Howard 393 (1857).
15. 12 Howard 299 (1851).
16. Remini, *Henry Clay,* 508–11; *Congressional Globe,* 25 Cong., 2 sess., appendix, 578–60.
17. *Congressional Globe,* 25 Cong., 2 sess., 199, 218, 328–32.
18. *Rice v Ballard,* discussed in Catterall, ed., *Judicial Cases Concerning American Slavery,* 3:278–79, 533–37.

7. OVERVIEW

1. There is an interesting itemized list of his legal materials in *CP*, 2:912–13.
2. When he left his service as secretary of state in 1829, following the defeat of President John Quincy Adams for reelection, he inclined not to return to a law practice and remarked, "I have not determined to return to the practice of my old profession, and nothing but necessity will compel me to put on the harness again. That I hope to be able to avoid." Colton, ed., *Private Correspondence,* 233. But generally, his correspondence demonstrated a very positive view of his law practice.
3. Clay to Jesse Burton Harrison, Sept. 11, 1831, *CP*, 8:399–401.
4. Clay to Charles Lanman, Oct. 28, 1817, ibid., 2:393.

5. Clay to Henry Clay Jr., Apr. 20, 1831, *CP*, 8:329, is a typical letter to his son.

6. Hall, *Magic Mirror*, 106–28, provides an informative view of legal history during the years of Clay's practice.

SELECTED BIBLIOGRAPHY

Abernethy, Thomas P. *The Burr Conspiracy.* New York, 1954.

Adams, John Quincy. *Memoirs of John Quincy Adams.* Ed. by Charles F. Adams. Vol. 6. Philadelphia, 1875.

Baker, Leonard. *John Marshall: A Life in Law.* New York, 1974.

Baxter, Maurice G. *Daniel Webster and the Supreme Court.* Amherst, Mass., 1966.

———. *Henry Clay and the American System.* Lexington, Ky., 1995.

———. *One and Inseparable: Daniel Webster and the Union.* Cambridge, Mass.,1984.

Beirne, Francis F. *Shout Treason: The Trial of Aaron Burr.* New York,1959.

Beveridge, Albert J. *The Life of John Marshall.* 4 vols. Boston, 1916–1919.

Bogart, Ernest L. "Taxation of the Second Bank of the United States by Ohio." *American Historical Review* 17 (Jan. 1912): 312–31.

Buley, R. Carlyle. *The Old Northwest: Pioneer Period, 1815–40.* Bloomington, Ind., 1951.

Burns, Francis P. "Henry Clay Visits New Orleans." *Louisiana Historical Quarterly* 27 (July 1944): 717–82.

Catterall, Helen T., ed. *Judicial Cases Concerning American Slavery and the Negro.* Vol. 3, *Cases from the Courts of Georgia, Florida, Alabama, Mississippi, and Louisiana.* Washington, D.C., 1932.

Cheetham, Jean Dick. "State Sovereignty in Ohio." *Ohio Archeological and Historical Society Publications* 9 (1901): 290–302.

Clay, Cassius M. *The Life of Cassius Marcellus Clay.* Cincinnati, 1886.

Coleman, Peter J. *Debtors and Creditors in America: Insolvency, Imprisonment for Debt, and Bankruptcy, 1607–1900.* Madison, Wis., 1874.

Colton, Calvin, ed. *The Life, Correspondence, and Speeches of Henry Clay.* 6 vols. New York, 1857.

———. *The Private Correspondence of Henry Clay.* Cincinnati, 1856.

Connelley, William E., and E. Merton Coulter. *History of Kentucky.* Edited by Charles Kerr. 5 vols. Chicago, 1922.

Currie, David P. *The Constitution in the Supreme Court: The First Hundred Years, 1789–1888.* Chicago, 1985.

Daveiss, Joseph Hamilton. *"A View of the President's Conduct Concerning the Conspiracy of 1806."* Edited by Isaac J. Cox and Helen A. Swineford. *Quarterly Publications of the Historical Society of Ohio* 12 (1917):58–154. First published contemporaneously as a pamphlet.

Dowd, Morgan D. "Justice Story, the Supreme Court, and the Obligation of Contract." *Case Western Reserve Law Review* 19 (1968): 493–529.

Duff, John J. *A. Lincoln: Prairie Lawyer.* New York, 1960.

Eaton, Clement. *Henry Clay and the Art of American Politics.* Boston, 1957.

Ellis, Richard E. *The Jeffersonian Crisis: Courts and Politics in the Young Republic.* New York, 1971.

Fitch, Raymond E., ed. *Breaking with Burr: Harman Blennerhassett's Journal, 1807.* Athens, Ohio, 1988.

Frank, John P. *Lincoln as a Lawyer.* Urbana, Ill., 1961.

Frankfurter, Felix, and James M. Landis. "The Compact Clause of the Constitution: A Study in Interstate Adjustments." *Yale Law Journal* 34 (1925): 685–758.

Freyer, Tony A. *Producers versus Capitalists: Constitutional Conflict in Antebellum America.* Charlottesville, Va., 1994.

Friedman, Lawrence M. *A History of American Law.* 2nd ed. New York, 1985.

Friedman, Lawrence M., and Harry N. Scheiber, eds. *American Law and the Constitutional Order: Historical Perspectives.* Cambridge, Mass., 1978.

Gates, Paul W. "Tenants of the Log Cabin." *Mississippi Valley Historical Review* 49 (June 1962): 3–31.

Haar, Charles M., ed. *The Golden Age of American Law*. New York, 1965.

Haines, Charles G. *The Role of the Supreme Court in American Government and Politics, 1789–1835*. Berkeley, Calif., 1944.

Haines, Charles G., and Foster H. Sherwood. *The Role of the Supreme Court in American Government and Politics, 1835–1864*. Berkeley, Calif., 1957.

Hall, Kermit. *The Magic Mirror: Law in American History*. New York, 1989.

Hall, Kermit, William Wiecek, and Paul Finkelman. *American Legal History: Cases and Materials*. New York, 1991.

Hammond, Bray. *Banks and Politics in America from the Revolution to the Civil War*. Princeton, N.J., 1957.

Holt, Michael. *The Political Crisis of the 1850s*. New York, 1978.

Hopkins, James F., et al., eds. *The Papers of Henry Clay*. 11 vols. Lexington, Ky., 1959–92.

Horwitz, Morton J. *The Transformation of American Law, 1780–1860*. Cambridge, Mass., 1977.

Huntington, C.C. "A History of Banking and Currency in Ohio before the Civil War." *Ohio Archeological and Historical Society Publications* 24 (1915): 235–539.

Hyman, Harold M., and William M. Wiecek. *Equal Justice under Law: Constitutional Development, 1835–75*. New York, 1982.

Jacobs, Clyde. *The Eleventh Amendment and Sovereign Immunity*. Westport, Conn., 1972.

Jillson, Willard R. *Henry Clay's Defense of Aaron Burr in 1806: An Episode of Early Western Adventure*. Frankfort, Ky., 1943.

Jillson, Willard R., ed. *The Kentucky Land Grants: a Systemic Index to All of the Land Grants Recorded in the State Land Office at Frankfort, Kentucky, 1782–1924*. Filson Club Publications, no.33. Louisville, 1925.

Johnson, Herbert A. *The Chief Justiceship of John Marshall, 1801–35*. Columbia, S.C., 1997.

Kelly, Alfred H., Winfred A. Harbison, and Herman Belz. *The American Constitution*. 6th ed. New York, 1991.

Konefsky, Alfred S. and Andrew J. King, eds. *The Papers of Daniel Webster, Legal Papers*. Vol.3, *The Federal Practice*, edited by Andrew J. King. Hanover, N.H., 1989.

Lomask, Milton. *Aaron Burr: The Conspiracy and Years of Exile, 1805–36*. 2 vols. New York, 1982.

Mayo, Bernard. *Henry Clay: Spokesman of the New West.* Boston, 1937.

McCaleb, Walter. *The Aaron Burr Conspiracy.* Expanded ed. New York, 1936.

McLaughlin, Andrew. *A Constitutional History of the United States.* New York, 1935.

Mikkelson, Dwight. "The *Kentucky Gazette,* 1787–1848." Ph. D. diss., University of Kentucky, 1963.

Mushkat, Jerome, and Joseph G. Rayback. *Martin Van Buren: Law, Politics, and the Shaping of Republican Ideology.* Dekalb, Ill., 1997.

Nelson, William E. *Americanization of the Common Law: The Impact of Legal Change in Massachusetts Society, 1760–1830.* Cambridge, Mass., 1975.

Newmyer, R. Kent. *The Supreme Court under Marshall and Taney.* New York, 1968.

———. *Supreme Court Justice Joseph Story: Statesman of the Old Republic.* Chapel Hill, N.C., 1985.

Niles' Weekly Register. Baltimore, 1821–1841.

Orth, John V. *The Judicial Power of the United States: The Eleventh Amendment in American History.* New York, 1987.

Pound, Roscoe. *The Formative Era of American Law.* Gloucester, Mass., 1938.

Prentice, George D. *Biography of Henry Clay.* Hartford, 1831.

Remini, Robert V. *Daniel Webster: The Man and His Time.* New York, 1997.

———. *Henry Clay: Statesman for the Union.* New York, 1991.

Roche, John P., ed. *John Marshall: Major Opinions and Other Writings.* Indianapolis, 1967.

Royalty, Dale M. "Banking, Politics, and the Commonwealth: Kentucky, 1800–1825." Ph.D. diss., University of Kentucky, 1971.

Sargent, Epes. *The Life and Public Services of Henry Clay.* New York, 1852.

Schachner, Nathan. *Aaron Burr.* New York, 1937.

Smelser, Marshall. *The Democratic Republic, 1801–1815.* New York, 1968.

Smiley, David L. *Lion of White Hall: The Life of Cassius M. Clay.* Madison, Wis., 1962.

Smith, Jean Edward. *John Marshall: Definer of a Nation.* New York, 1996.

Stevens, Harry R. "Henry Clay, the Bank, and the West in 1824." *American Historical Review* 60 (July 1955): 843–48.

Stites, Francis N. *John Marshall: Defender of the Constitution*. Boston, 1981.

Swisher, Carl B. *History of the Supreme Court of the United States*. Vol. 5, *The Taney Period, 1836–64*. New York, 1974.

———. *Roger B. Taney*. New York, 1935.

Urofsky, Melvin I. *A March of Liberty: A Constitutional History of the United States*. New York, 1988.

Van Deusen, Glyndon G. *The Life of Henry Clay*. Boston, 1937.

Warren, Charles. *Bankruptcy in United States History*. Cambridge, Mass., 1935.

———. *The Supreme Court in United States History*. 3 vols. Boston, 1926.

White, G. Edward. *The Marshall Court and Cultural Change, 1815–35*. Vols.3–4 of *History of the Supreme Court of the United States*. New York, 1988.

Wilson, Samuel L., ed. "The Court Proceedings of 1806 in Kentucky against Aaron Burr and John Adair." *Filson Club Historical Quarterly* 10 (Jan. 1936): 31–40.

Wright, Benjamin F., Jr. *The Contract Clause of the Constitution*. Cambridge, Mass., 1938.

INDEX